LANDSCAPE AND SETTLEMENT IN BRITAIN AD 400–1066

EXETER STUDIES IN HISTORY
General Editors: Jonathan Barry, Tim Rees
and T.P. Wiseman

Also in the Exeter Studies in History series:

The Inheritance of Historiography, 350–900,
edited by Christopher Holdsworth and T. P. Wiseman (1986)

Security and Defence in South West England before 1800,
edited by Robert Higham (1987)

Landscape and Townscape in the South West,
edited by Robert Higham (1989)

The Saxon Shore: A handbook,
edited by Valerie Maxfield (1989)

LANDSCAPE AND SETTLEMENT IN BRITAIN AD 400–1066

Edited by

DELLA HOOKE *and* SIMON BURNELL

UNIVERSITY
of
EXETER
PRESS

First published in 1995 by
University of Exeter Press
Reed Hall, Streatham Drive
Exeter, Devon EX4 4QR
UK

British Library Cataloguing in Publication Data
A catalogue record of this book is available
from the British Library

ISBN 0 85989 386 3

Typeset in 11/12.5 Stempel Garamond
by Exe Valley Dataset Ltd, Exeter
Printed and bound in Great Britain
by BPC Wheatons Ltd, Exeter

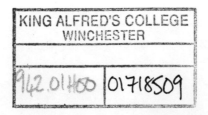

CONTENTS

LIST OF ILLUSTRATIONS

Cover picture—Stepping Stones, Meavy, Dartmoor: the *cleaca* of an eleventh-century charter boundary clause.

NOTES ON CONTRIBUTORS

COLLEEN BATEY graduated from the University of Durham in Archaeology in 1978 and completed her PhD there on the subject of Viking and Late Norse settlement in Caithness. Subsequently, she has worked on several major settlement sites in Northern Scotland and has published extensively on artefactural and ecofactural study of the Late Norse period. Following lecturing posts at the University of Leeds and University College London, she has held the post of Curator of Archaeology at Glasgow Museums since 1990.

JAMES BOND graduated from the University of Birmingham as an historical geographer. After working as an archaeological officer in the county museum services of Worcestershire (1969–74) and Oxfordshire (1974–86) he moved to north Somerset, where he now works as a freelance landscape archaeologist and part-time tutor with Bristol University Department for Continuing Education. He has published numerous articles on aspects of medieval settlement and landscape, and his current research interests are focussed upon the landscape of monastic estates.

SIMON BURNELL read Modern History at Merton College Oxford, and gained his DPhil in European Archaeology from the same university in 1989. He was Lecturer in Early Medieval Archaeology at the University of Exeter from 1990 to 1992, and has since taught at the Universities of Berne and Zurich. He works as a freelance research archaeologist and is based in Suffolk.

SIMON ESMONDE CLEARY read Archaeology at the Institute of Archaeology, University of London, and completed his DPhil at New College, Oxford. He is now Senior Lecturer in the Department of Ancient History and Archaeology in the University of Birmingham. He is the author of *The Ending of Roman Britain*

(Batsford, London, 1989) and numerous articles on Roman Britain with a particular interest in the transition from Roman to post-Roman Britain and Late Antiquity in the western Roman Empire.

CHRISTOPHER HOLDSWORTH is Professor of Medieval History at the University of Exeter. He has published widely on monasticism, including four volumes of the Rufford Charters for the Thoroton Society, Nottingham (1972–81), and is at present writing a book on Bernard of Clairvaux. He is interested also in the history of the South West and in medieval archaeology.

DELLA HOOKE graduated from the University of Birmingham Department of Geography and returned there to complete a PhD on Anglo-Saxon Landscapes of the West Midlands, the Charter Evidence, in 1980. She has subsequently published three county volumes of charters, with three others approaching completion, but her wider interests include aspects of settlement and land use change and the assessment and conservation of historical landscapes. Formerly a Research Fellow in the University of Birmingham she is now a Senior Lecturer in the Department of Geography and Geology in Cheltenham and Gloucester College of Higher Education and also works as a freelance consultant.

ANN PRESTON-JONES is based in the Cornwall Archaeological Unit of Cornwall County Council and is English Heritage's Field Monument Warden for Cornwall. Her interests include pre-Norman church enclosure, place-names and settlement in medieval Cornwall. the latter is a theme upon which she and Peter Rose have published a comprehensive study in *Cornish Archaeology* (1986).

PETER ROSE is the Senior Field Officer for the Cormwall Archaeological Unit of Cornwall County Council. He has published numerous papers on the archaeology of the South-West and has recently completed, with Nicholas Johnson and other contributors, the first volume of RCHME's archaeological survey of Bodmin Moor (1994). The historic character of the landscape is a particular interest.

FOREWORD

The papers collected in this volume, with the exception of the last chapter, are based on talks given at a conference on developments within the British landscape 400–1066, organized by the student Archaeological Society at the University of Exeter in December 1990. Without the work of Sally and Jim Navin, in particular, this project would never have got under way. Editing of this volume was begun by Dr Simon Burnell and then, when he moved to Switzerland for academic reasons, continued by Della Hooke. The series editors are grateful to both of them, and especially to the latter, who brought renewed vigour to the project and also arranged for James Bond to supply the final chapter in place of some of the papers which were given at the conference but which, for various reasons, the authors felt unable to include in this volume. To those original participants who have waited patiently for this volume to appear, we express our thanks. Thanks are also due to the technical staff of the Drawing Office in the Department of History and Archaeology, notably Mike Rouillard, who revised and prepared the figures for publication and offered much useful advice, and to Mick Aston and Bob Higham for comments on the essays.

Jonathan Barry, Timothy Rees and T. P. Wiseman
(Series Editors)

INTRODUCTION

Della Hooke

The aim of this volume is to explore, in a critical fashion, the way that perceptions of early medieval settlement and land use have changed over the last few decades. Not only has the documentary evidence been reassessed in the light of present knowledge but archaeology, in all its facets, has continued to provide additional information about the period.

There are still gaps in the record which can only be filled as individual case studies contribute additional information and as archaeological techniques are extended to new areas. It is not only a question of the *quantity* of data but the *quality* of research. Some of the more modern archaeological techniques may be expected to provide valuable information hitherto scarce: geophysical surveys may, for instance, supplement below-ground excavation comparatively cheaply, while study of environmental evidence is now an essential part of any detailed excavation project. Above all, the landscape has not yet yielded all its secrets but the skills of multidisciplinary research and a high degree of expertise are required to take this understanding further.

The volume begins with a study of the end of Roman Britain. In the middle years of this century the traumatic events of the Anglo-Saxon *conquest* were usually given prominence. To the peasant farmer of eastern England whose stock was taken to feed marauding armies and who had to witness his crops burnt and perhaps members of his family killed, the events of the later fifth century were indeed catastrophic. Many more were inevitably hit by the hardships which accompanied a breakdown in the economic organization of late Roman Britain, and archaeology seems to depict a general lowering of living standards at the very least. Those who lived in urban environments by craft or trade no longer had a surrounding rural populace willing or able to maintain them. But farming did continue and Simon Esmonde Cleary summarizes the situation as he now sees it in Chapter 1.

The landscape remained peopled but changing burial rites mean that the dead become less visible in the archaeological record; so, too, the living, occupying buildings which were reverting to native tradition and perhaps with less expression of differences in the social hierarchy. Farming was released from its burden of producing a surplus for the support of the army, the bureaucracy, the aristocracy and the townsfolk of late Roman Britain, so there were inevitably changes, with marginal lands, in particular, going out of production. Native farming methods, perhaps with more emphasis on cattle rearing, may have come once again to the fore and Bourdillon (1988) has noted how the quality of domestic stock remained high throughout the early medieval period.

Esmonde Cleary carries his study of the changing economic and social structure of what was formerly known as 'Dark Age Britain' into the sixth and early seventh centuries when an established aristocracy again becomes visible, its rise reflected in princely burials, 'palace' ranges and a complex pattern of kingdoms and folk units. The simplistic notion of cataclysm is rejected and instead he argues for changes of emphasis in the use of the landscape, reflecting 'the culture and habits of the people who lived off it' (p. 24). He reveals how much information on social hierarchy, for instance, can be gleaned from a skilful interpretation of the archaeological record.

Ethnicity alone has been questioned as the dominant factor influencing change. As Nick Higham, in a recently published study, concludes: 'Whatever else, the retention or abandonment of enclosed landscapes do not seem to have been matters which were decided on the basis of ethnicity or migration'. Changes can be explained 'without recourse to the theories of large-scale immigration and population replacement which have tended to be popular explanations of this evidence' (Higham 1992, pp. 134, 119).

But changes there certainly were, not least in language: and here archaeology must give way to the evidence of the historical documentation and place-names. Some authorities play down the role of the Anglo-Saxon invaders, both in the numbers involved and in the impact they had upon the native population; others have argued that the numbers of Anglo-Saxons entering the country must have been huge to explain the almost total language change that occurred by the seventh century. It is likely that further evidence will be derived from the new field of genetic enquiry but the Anglo-Saxons were of mixed race when they entered the country.

Old English, the language of the Anglo-Saxons, had a number of features which contributed to its success. Firstly, it was the language of what was to become the dominant race. Similarly, when explorers moved to the New World the first thing they did was to re-christen the places at which they landed. By doing this, a linguistic authority was established and a place appropriated for the new ruling race. Second, the new language maintained group identity and power, a process deliberately encouraged among those wishing to strengthen nationalistic feeling today. Third, and an equally powerful factor, was the fact that the Anglo-Saxons, at least in the royal courts and in the church, made increasing use of documentation to record legal transactions, especially those concerning land. Admittedly Latin was the language used for official documentation, but the newly recorded place-names which were written down for the first time were Old English and, once written down, were less likely to change. Furthermore, English became the language of trade and anyone who wished to participate in this had to master it.

Yet it may give food for thought that where a population continued to communicate in home and field in its own tongue, as the British might have been expected to do, that language seldom disappeared. Welsh remained pre-eminent in Wales despite the

Edwardian conquest and strong attempts later to ban its use in schools; Cornwall was not fully assimilated into England until the tenth century and the Cornish language was spoken until recent times, with Cornish place-names surviving throughout the county. In both these cases the native language was not eradicated by newcomers. Neither did the Norman-French overlay of post-Conquest England produce a noticeable change in everyday speech patterns. While the numbers of Anglo-Saxons entering the country have yet to be assessed, the linguistic change may have been encouraged by the fact that they appear to have penetrated at all levels of the social hierarchy.

What is still to be established, however, are the effects such immigration had upon land use and settlement. No single volume could attempt to explore the variations in patterns that were present across early medieval England. In some areas early field systems apparently continued in use while in others they had been eradicated by the end of the Anglo-Saxon period. Much of this was due to the adoption of open field agriculture, a feature well represented in a band across south-central, midland and parts of eastern England. Associated closely with changing field layouts, the period witnessed the beginnings of a move towards settlement nucleation in these same regions but, as with the agricultural changes, these do not seem to gather momentum until late in the period in question. Given this fact, which seems to be supported by the environmental evidence so far available, such changes can no longer be attributed to innovations brought in 'ready-made' by the conquering Anglo-Saxons.

There were, however, changes in administrative organization and, probably, changes in land tenure and attitudes to ownership that are less easily investigated by archaeology. These, again, may not have been confined to particular ethnic groupings and can certainly be paralleled on the Continent. In addition, similarities between Celtic (British) and Anglo-Saxon institutions have also been identified. These can be particularly recognized at the beginning of the period, such as in the perception of the hide (Charles Edwards 1972), but many similarities between Welsh and English systems persist in later centuries, among them systems of transhumance or the development of multiple estates. Even the subdivision of territories such as minster *parochiae* into individual parish units was clearly advanced in Cornwall by the tenth century, and individual estates were recognized as early as the sixth century in South Wales (Davies 1978). Territorial subdivision was to take place across the country as the Anglo-Saxon period progressed, both on a secular and ecclesiastical level, giving rise to the parish patterns which remained the basic units of administration for nearly a thousand years.

Christianity had been a powerful force in late Roman Britain and Christopher Holdsworth reviews the expression of this faith anew in England from the late sixth century in Chapter 2. He explores the reasons for Christian leaders choosing established centres for the sees of bishoprics. He notes the advantages offered by an urban environment but also considers what other factors may have led to a place retaining its role as a sacred centre. Minsters, too, were founded in a variety of different sites: some remote and rural, others central-place locations. The necessity for sufficient land and resources to provide for the upkeep of the monastery and its inhabitants, especially by the tenth century, is a factor which has not always been fully appreciated hitherto. The effect of the Church upon social institutions has been well researched by historians but the economic implications of its organization were tremendous, influencing the manipulation of resources to an extent still not fully investigated.

In Chapter 3 Peter Rose and Ann Preston-Jones present the evidence from Cornwall, one of the regions least affected by the Anglo-Saxon take-over. Here, one might expect rather more continuity in the rural landscape. Surprisingly, perhaps, they find rather more evidence of dislocation at the beginning of the period than Esmonde Cleary's arguments would seem to warrant. Some explanation must be found for a general retraction in the extent and density of settlement as evidenced by archaeology and place-names. This was apparently followed, later, by fresh expansion onto more marginal land. They tentatively reconstruct for a number of regions a pattern of rectilinear field systems associated with scattered settlements which in some locations were amalgamated into the present field pattern but in others totally disregarded by present-day fields. The latter areas seem to be the ones of most severe settlement abandonment, as elsewhere a process frequently affecting the more marginal land. In seeking reasons for settlement retraction and for changing styles of settlement construction they consider political, social and economic changes which may have been taking place in the fifth and sixth centuries. The political upheavals may, for instance, have affected the prosperity of the tin industry. Yet, if change is a feature apparent in the countryside there remains still a greater degree of continuity here than that found in many other parts of the country. Medieval and earlier settlement patterns are sufficiently related for direct comparisons in distribution patterns to be made and the field patterns of the region still contain vestiges of earlier fieldscapes that can be reconstructed by topographical technique. The methods used here by Rose and Preston-Jones are obviously of considerable potential.

Chapter 4 carries the investigation to a very different part of the country: northern Britain. In a detailed study of house types across the region, Colleen Batey looks at the feasibility of using archaeological techniques to identify ethnic change, in this case trying to define Scandinavian influence. She attempts to identify a specific Scandinavian house type but is forced to conclude that 'archaeology itself cannot yet always identify the foreigner, especially not if that foreigner is content to continue local traditions. It is only the innovator who can really be identified in the archaeological record.' Nevertheless, the excavated sites offer valuable information about the kind of small, upland farmstead of the period that has only rarely been investigated, and detailed studies bring us closer to an understanding of how people really lived in such an environment. Environmental archaeology also confirms that the landscape of many northern areas was as treeless in the early medieval period as it is today and that the builders had recourse to limited timber supplies but readily available stone or rubble and turf.

In Chapter 5, Hooke reviews the evidence for agricultural change in the early medieval period and considers some of the reasons for its occurrence. Estate fragmentation which forced each township community to become relatively self-sufficient is seen as a powerful factor, entailing as it did changing attitudes to land ownership and the thegnly control of individual manors. The emphasis in this chapter is perhaps more upon lordly control than the self-motivation of peasant communities. Some of the earliest signs of settlement planning seem to appear on royal estates or those of other powerful bodies such as the Church. This does not represent the views of all present-day historians but the factual evidence so far leaves ample room for hypothesis. Increasing subordination of the peasantry may have been the gradual but natural outcome of the more intensive exploitation of the smaller estate unit; it has long been known that the peasantry generally enjoyed greater freedom in less heavily exploited regions (Everitt 1986; Roberts 1968).

The same chapter examines those regions in which dispersed settlement patterns remained dominant. In some parts of the country this does seem to perpetuate an older pattern of settlement, as evidenced in the chapter by Rose and Preston-Jones dealing with Cornwall. Hooke notes the dangers of interpreting the nature of early medieval settlement sites from later evidence, showing how numerous individual homesteads could readily be subsumed under a single surviving place-name. The example quoted is taken from Wales but similar evidence can be found throughout upland Britain.

Given that hundreds of years of continuous cultivation may have virtually eradicated many of the field patterns of early Anglo-Saxon England, studies in marginal areas may often reveal more than those in heavily settled zones. The chapters by Rose and Preston-Jones, Batey and Hooke all to a degree use their different techniques to explore regions which were marginal to a greater or lesser extent and far from the mainstream of Anglo-Saxon cultural evidence: the south-west of England, the northern uplands or well-wooded regions away from the main areas of cultivation. Against the use of such areas for an investigation into changing (or unchanging) practices of land use is the fact that these areas were marginal. Some settlements, including some of those examined by Batey on the flanks of the Pennines, may even have been largely of seasonal use.

It is appropriate for the final chapter of the book to concentrate upon a specific case study. In such a study there is no escape from those elements of land use and settlement for which evidence is lacking or which are only partially understood. James Bond has chosen to concentrate upon the development of land use and estate patterns on the Failand ridge in north Somerset and here the problems of understanding the early medieval period are set within a much broader timescale. He reviews the development of the area through the prehistoric period, with a number of hillforts dominating a pattern of smaller individual enclosures, some of which were to continue in use in Roman times. The higher parts of the ridge were again of marginal character but the Iron Age hillforts appear to have seen reuse as pagan sanctuaries towards the latter part of the Roman period, a period when villas were being established on lower ground. The settlement evidence is set against what is known about the contemporary environment, with arable receding from the ridge top to give way to permanent pasture by the Middle Ages. Stands of ancient woodland survived on the steeper slopes on either side of the ridge, subject in places to local medieval clearance for agriculture; some were to be enclosed within medieval deer parks. Below, open field extended across the lower ground, some of it enclosed piecemeal, probably during the sixteenth and seventeenth centuries. Finally, the moors provided summer grazing and opportunities for fishing and fowling until relatively recent times.

This is a relatively stable pattern of land use, similar to that noted in many regions throughout southern England (Hooke 1988), but settlement was 'remarkably fluid' and Bond's study offers a warning to those disinclined to recognize the frequency of settlement shift that might take place at any time within the medieval or post-medieval period. He is also critical about attempts to see unproven continuity in territorial boundaries. Thus the limitations of present-day knowledge remain apparent, but at least we now view them with healthy scepticism and a realization of our inability to provide 'definitive answers'. Readers may judge the potential of the techniques available to historians, archaeologists and historical geographers attempting to reconstruct past landscapes: each has a role to play and these chapters show how the various approaches are interrelated.

Recurrent themes that appear in these pages include discussion of the physical components of the landscape of the period: its settlements and their surrounding fields, and the related use of pasture, moor and woodland, producing patterns that can still be discerned in the landscape of today. Certainly man's use of the land had to be adapted to the nature of the underlying geology and soils, the local climatic conditions and the natural resources available, but these factors would encourage a greater continuity of land use than has always been discovered. While avoiding the stress placed upon determinism in many of the early works of this century, it may not be wrong to suggest that such natural factors indeed provided a certain propensity for the relative constancy of land use remarked upon by several contributors. The use of marginal land especially, however, has obviously been affected by fluctuating economic and social conditions. But physical characteristics are not always dominant: territories, settlements and actual field systems reflect the administrative, social and economic climate which shaped them and it is in these components of the landscape that change is most apparent. The early medieval period was undoubtedly a formative period in English history: settlements might be abandoned, left to seasonal use or re-established, often on quite different sites and conforming to different patterns; new field systems might be introduced with old ones being either adapted or abandoned; territories were constantly re-shaped in response to changing social conditions and administrative systems. Such change has, however, to be viewed against a much wider timescale, as several of the contributors to this volume clearly illustrate.

One of the most important conclusions is that the landscape can still offer so much to the discerning eye. In a period when change is occurring more rapidly than ever before, it is the greatest surviving asset to historical research that we have.

References

Bourdillon, J., 1988. 'Countryside and town: the animal resources of Saxon Southampton', in *Anglo-Saxon Settlements*, ed. D. Hooke (Oxford), pp. 176–95.

Charles Edwards, T.M., 1972. 'Kinship, status and the origins of the hide', *Past and Present*, 56, pp. 3–33.

Davies, W., 1978. *An Early Welsh Microcosm* (London).

Everitt, A., 1986. *Continuity and Colonization. The Evolution of Kentish Settlement* (Leicester).

Higham, N., 1992. *Rome, Britain and the Anglo-Saxons* (London).

Hooke, D., 1988. 'Regional variation in southern and central England in the Anglo-Saxon period and its relationship to land units and settlement', in *Anglo-Saxon Settlements*, ed. D. Hooke (Oxford), pp. 123–51.

Roberts, B.K., 1968. 'A study of medieval colonization in the Forest of Arden, Warwickshire', *Agricultural History Review*, 16, pp. 101–13.

CHAPTER ONE

Changing Constraints on the Landscape AD 400–600

Simon Esmonde Cleary

'Landscape' is often a rather imprecise concept in archaeological literature. Ideally, of course, it refers to the totality of natural and man-made elements which make up an area at any one time. But because of an understandable bias in favour of positive over negative evidence, archaeologists often slip into the practice of equating the surviving evidence for settlements, fields, tracks and the like with 'the landscape'. I wish to argue here that this ambiguity has underlain much of the discussion of the landscape in the period which is of concern here, but that if we keep the various categories of evidence distinct we can come up with a more rounded and interesting view of what was going on in the landscape, and why. The discussion will be almost entirely about the area that is now England, not only because it makes sense in the Anglo-Saxon period but also because it was the heartland of Roman Britain.

A landscape is the result of the interaction between natural resources and the modifications and demands wrought upon them by humans. Among the most important natural features are climate, relief, geology, soils and drainage. To these humans added the modified natural resources of domesticated plants and animals with their requirements for space and nutrients. Humans also modify the natural environment by the impedimenta of their management of crops and herds: fields, tracks, boundaries (physical and tenurial), to which must be added the structures and settlements of human habitation. All these are pretty much ubiquitous in Britain from the Neolithic period onwards (if differentially represented by period). Each period also tends to add a superstructure of specialized, relatively uncommon sites, be they henges, hillforts, towns or castles. These latter are important because they are all agriculturally redundant and depend on being able to extract surplus from the agricultural landscape.

The relationship between natural and human components in a landscape is not of course static, it is dynamic. Changes in any of the natural parameters can alter the agricultural potential of the land, for good or ill. Sometimes these changes are beyond human initiation or control, for instance in the case of climate change. Sometimes it is human activity which initiates and effects this change, for instance in the deforestation of areas of nutrient-poor and unstable soils with their rapid erosion, leaching and consequent loss to arable and conversion to heath or scrub. Human influences can vary in other ways, for instance with the introduction of new implements or crops, and particularly in the intensification or slackening of demand.

The period under discussion in this chapter is one which sees one of the sharpest breaks in the archaeological sequence in England, one which in its turn has spawned one of the deepest divisions in modern archaeological specialisms. Briefly, a highly visible and famous civilization, the Roman, disappears totally; a 'Dark Age' ensues; out of this eventually emerge the origins of Anglo-Saxon England. What we find in the literary or archaeological evidence at the end of the period seems to have almost nothing to do with that for the beginning of the period. In the middle, evidence almost entirely fails us. Such a cultural cataclysm and reworking has often been assumed to have involved all aspects of human endeavour, including agricultural exploitation and thence the form of the landscape. This was reflected in the commonly-held view, sanctioned in such works of popular scholarship as W.G. Hoskins' *The Making of the English Landscape* (Hoskins 1955), that the immediate post-Roman period saw demographic collapse leading to huge areas of previously farmed land falling out of cultivation and reverting to forest. It was out of this woodland that the Anglo-Saxons hacked their new landscape, a process witnessed in the *-lēah* place-names, betokening woods or clearings (cf. Gelling 1984, pp. 198–207 for a more subtle analysis). Sometimes it is difficult to distinguish whether this population and agrarian collapse was the supposed cause or the effect of the end of Romano-British culture.

It is worth pausing on these proposed collapses and considering whether they have any more value than as a *deus ex machina*. Both of them essentially seek to establish external factors beyond human control and so overwhelming as to explain the cultural break by themselves. The hypothesis of population collapse rests partly on the mentions of pestilence and plague in Gildas (*De Excidio* §§2,22), partly on the paucity of the archaeological evidence for the post-Roman centuries and partly on the evidence from the time of Domesday that the population was increasing but possibly still lower than at its late Roman peak. The validity of the evidence of Gildas has been challenged both on the grounds of what we know of the incidence of plague in this period (Todd 1977) and of its appearance in a work of Christian polemic rather than of historical narrative (cf. Esmonde Cleary 1989, pp. 166–67). The question of the level of archaeological evidence and its meaning will be the central concern of a later part of this essay where it will be argued that it is explicable in other, human, terms. The Domesday evidence is more convincing. I have no wish to deny that the population may have contracted in the post-Roman period; my feeling is that it did, but independent and quantifiable evidence is lacking. But even if one were to cling to the hypothesis of sudden population decline and/or plague, there remains the question of whether this is convincing as an explanation of culture collapse, particularly taking into account the evidence of better-documented pandemics in the ancient and medieval worlds.

What of climate change? That climate has fluctuated throughout the post-glacial period is a truism, and one that is now uncomfortably topical. That sometimes these fluctuations were pronounced enough to bring measurable deterioration (or amelioration) in the conditions for agriculture is again undoubted. There is evidence for some climatic deterioration in northern Europe through late antiquity, with a move to cooler and wetter conditions. In Britain this seems to have affected areas such as Wales (cf. Davies 1982, Ch. 2). But agriculturally much of Wales was always marginal, since its relief, soils and drainage conspire to ensure that only slight climatic deterioration can have pronounced effects. More important in this discussion is whether the deterioration was pronounced enough to affect the productivity of southern, midland and eastern England, the bread-basket of Britain. To do that would have required a downturn far greater than that for which we have evidence. Indeed, the evidence to be discussed below for agricultural continuity in England argues strongly against climatically-induced collapse. And as with population collapse, there remains the question of whether and how any such climatic deterioration would bring about the observed cultural changes of the fifth and sixth centuries.

If the traditional view of a collapse of the British population is untenable, is there anything we can put in its place? I would argue that what is needed is to return to the idea of distinguishing between the various elements of the landscape and examining them in the crucial period of transition, centring on the fifth century. It has just been argued that the natural elements of the landscape did not change significantly at this period, in England at least. Undoubtedly there will have been local variations, some of them significant, but overall the picture seems to remain pretty constant. What then of the other elements? Here there are important indicators beginning to accumulate from three sources of evidence: pollen analysis; work on field and other boundaries; and the study of grain and animal bones as evidence for arable and pastoral regimes.

The mid-first millennium AD has not been a principal concern of pollen analysts, but some cores do cover the period and the evidence has recently been reviewed by Bell (1989) and Turner (1981). The most important result of this work is to show that far from there having been an agrarian collapse and a relapse to forest, the immediate post-Roman period sees no significant increase in the amount of tree pollen and maintained levels of pollen of the plants of deforested land. The inescapable conclusion is that the landscape of England which had been largely deforested by the late Iron Age remained that way. Indeed, some of Turner's (1981) evidence from the north-east of England suggests that there deforestation not only continued into the Roman but also into the post-Roman period. Woodland regeneration may have been a phenomenon of the middle rather than the early Saxon period.

Work on the survival of field boundaries is now pointing in the same direction. It has been shown that in some areas of East Anglia (Williamson 1986, 1987) and the east and west Midlands (Bassett 1985, 1990) stretches of field layouts of likely late prehistoric or Romano-British date survive in the modern landscape. For this to have happened the fields in question must have remained in use through the fifth and sixth centuries, otherwise their boundaries would have been lost. Of course these only form a tiny percentage of the total landscape of England, but they are randomly distributed, suggesting that their survival is not tied to preferential soil or other such factors. Other such areas doubtless await identification.

Another type of boundary is that of a territory under a particular control or ownership. Steven Bassett has recently proposed (Bassett 1989, 1992) a number of areas in the western Midlands where such territories may perhaps be identified at an early date. Some of these, such as the equation of the minster parish of Wootton Wawen, Warwickshire, with the territory of a folk known as the *Stoppingas* (Bassett 1989, pp. 18–19), are of middle Saxon date. But others, he suggests, may betray origins in earlier, British contexts, taking them back into the period which is our concern. If this be so, then it points to a countryside which was sufficiently populated and open to be worth ordering in this way.

When we turn to the environmental evidence for the crops and herds being grown and raised in this period, the evidence is at present exiguous in the extreme. The evidence from the Romano-British period is considerably more extensive and is beginning to yield some sort of coherent structure (Grant 1989; Jones 1981, 1989; Maltby 1981). It seems to demonstrate a broad continuity from the Iron Age regime, with spelt wheat the dominant grain, along with emmer, barley and oats, as well as vegetables, legumes and herbs. The main animal species were cattle, sheep and pigs. It seems likely that changes took place in the Anglo-Saxon period in crop cultivation at least, with the rise to dominance of breadwheat. Fifth-century sites are at a premium. On the British (i.e. non-Anglo-Saxon) side there is, for instance, the settlement at Poundbury, Dorchester, Dorset (Sparey Green 1987). Whereas the animal bone assemblage is similar to that from Romano-British sites, the evidence of the carbonized grain is striking, for it demonstrates a switch away from spelt and towards the bread-wheats. On the other hand, the publication of the environmental evidence from the Anglo-Saxon site at West Stow, Suffolk (Crabtree 1991) has shown that the animal range is not greatly different to that from Romano-British sites. In terms of its material culture West Stow is a 'typical' Anglo-Saxon settlement (West 1985); the objects from it are of early Anglo-Saxon type and the structures are of the types usually found on Anglo-Saxon sites (though cf. James et al. 1984 for caution on their cultural provenance). But if we accept that the Anglo-Saxons were not arriving in a plague-stricken, re-afforesting landscape, it seems sensible that they should fit into the existing landscape with its own long-established agricultural regime. At first they adapted to it; only later did they adapt it.

If the arguments deployed above (and it is acknowledged that they vary greatly in the amount and reliability of the evidence) are conceded at least as a debating position, then certain conclusions follow. It would seem that by and large the landscape remained open and deforested. It remained in agricultural use, though not necessarily in precisely the same ways as it had been in the Roman period. There was also both continuity and change in the agrarian use, though not perhaps in the expected contexts.

It may at this point reasonably be objected that this is all very well as an example of the revisionism beloved of academics, but that there remains much good evidence for major changes in the archaeology of England between the end of the Roman and the beginning of the middle Saxon periods. Granted, there is such evidence, but it still needs to be assessed against some of the criteria outlined earlier on. First of all, which elements of the landscape is it with which we must deal here? They are essentially settlements, artefacts and cemeteries. I would argue that these are the elements of the landscape most closely allied to cultural and social patterns and to changes in those patterns, and that they need to be viewed in that light. They are also, of course, the types of evidence most visible and familiar to the archaeologist and are thus at risk of forming a disproportionate amount of the evidential basis. In part it is again the bias in favour of positive over negative or elusive evidence. Nevertheless, there is a significant amount and range of evidence, and it is the evidence which seems to argue most strongly for major changes in the landscape.

First of all we need to make explicit the changes which are observable in this period. This can be done by selecting three chronological/cultural horizons, characterizing the types of settlement, artefactual and funerary evidence from them, comparing these and then seeking explanations for them.

The archaeology of the late Roman period, say the mid to late fourth century, is almost overwhelming in its quantity and variety. Settlements are many and various. The bulk of the population lived on the land, the majority of them in the 'farmsteads' which in their layout and building types owed more to Iron Age British than to Mediterranean precedents. The aristocracy resided in its Roman-style villas, ranging in size from the palatial as at Bignor, to the piddling as at Barnack. The more well-to-do of these were decked out with mosaics, painted wall-plaster and hypocausts in the main residential blocks. Serving them was a variety of barns, byres and other outbuildings. In addition to the rural settlements there were the other types of settlement which help define the Roman period in Britain: the forts, the towns ('large' and 'small'), the temples and shrines, the extractive and manufacturing sites. Many of these, especially the forts, towns and villas, exhibit a range of structural types varying in complexity of plan and appointments and suggesting social and functional differentiation. Many of the buildings were built of relatively durable materials. The artefactual richness of most Romano-British sites is quasi-proverbial. There is a great variety in the materials employed and the techniques. There are precious and base metals, glass, textiles, wood, leather, pottery, bone, stone. The list is long but not as long as the list of different types of artefacts and their forms. The burial and cemetery evidence from Roman Britain has long been under-valued, but is now coming into its own (cf. Philpott 1991). For the late Roman period it shows a considerable quantity of burials south of the Humber-Mersey line, and a range of burial rites with regional, social and chronological variation (cf. Esmonde Cleary 1992). The Romano-British are very archaeologically visible.

To turn to the next chronological/cultural horizon is to encounter an almost complete contrast. By the mid to later fifth century in the British areas, archaeology almost entirely fails us. Settlements are few, because they are almost impossible to detect. We have already encountered Poundbury, almost the only example of its period. Had it not overlain the Romano-British cemetery which was the main aim of the excavation it is doubtful whether it would ever have been discovered, since its artefactual suite is limited and unremarkable. The structures at Poundbury were of wood and to a very simple plan. This lack of distinctive artefacts is undoubtedly a, if not the, major reason why sites of this period are so difficult to locate and identify; they lack distinguishing criteria. Even the dead are secretive. Few burials or cemeteries of this period have been identified in England (cf. Rahtz 1977), though the position is now improving for Wales (James 1992). It has been suggested that this was because, as in the Iron Age, an archaeologically-invisible burial rite was in use. But our evidence is that by the sixth century the British population was Christianized, and as the Church insisted on an archaeologically-visible burial rite it would seem likely that we should see inhumation burial as the majority rite in the fifth century. The problem is more likely to be one of identification. Lacking a suite of distinctive fifth-century British artefacts it is difficult to date burials (even if the church had permitted grave-goods). Another possibility is that burials of this period have been mis-identified as Anglo-Saxon because of the presence in them of objects of Anglo-Saxon type or manufacture (Esmonde Cleary 1989, p. 201). Clearly we have major problems of visibility and identification. It is not surprising that this was taken to mean a catastrophic drop in population. But given the high suggested population levels for late Roman Britain and the evidence for the landscape remaining open and worked in the fifth century, what we are facing is surely a population that archaeologists find difficult to locate, rather than a population that was not there in the first place.

To take the same chronological horizon but to move into the cultural area of the incoming Anglo-Saxons is to change archaeological emphasis once again. Settlements such as Mucking (Hamerow 1991) and West Stow (West 1985) with their 'hall' buildings and *grubenhäuser* suggest relatively nucleated farming settlements of family- or kin-groups. The cemetery evidence is not inconsistent with this. Though there are differences observable in the treatment of the dead according to factors such as age, gender or status (Härke 1990; Pader 1982), there is again little evidence for pronounced social stratification or hierarchy. Though there may be differences within individual settlements or cemeteries, there is relatively little variation in social status between settlements and cemeteries at this date. This was something which developed through the sixth and on into the seventh century. The range of artefacts, also, is relatively restricted when compared to the Roman period, though this is not to deny that in artistic or aesthetic terms some of them were of high quality, or that many were of precious metal or stones.

I would suggest that the differences we see here are essentially products of changes in social organization and its manifestations rather than of any intrinsic change in the landscape of Britain. In proposing explanations for this change it would seem that there are three linked strands: hierarchy, differentiation and modes of display. It is these three which can be seen changing from the late Roman period on. The mechanism which links these changes back to the landscape, and which we must examine here, is surplus extraction.

The late Roman period was characterized by a deep social hierarchy, a considerable amount of social differentiation and specialization, and a tradition of social display in forms which leave plenty of archaeological trace. All of these were dependent on a high level of surplus extraction from the rural population. From the literary and archaeological sources we can identify a number of different levels in the social hierarchy and some of the specialist groups within late Romano-British society. One of the most distinctive features of the late Roman Empire was its large standing army and its extensive bureaucracy (the latter existing largely to service the former). The army was supplied with most of its wants by the State. It was fed, clothed, equipped, armed, paid by the State. So too were the members of the civil service. This system required constant efforts by the State to raise the foodstuffs, raw materials and bullion on which all this depended. In large part this was through the taxation system. This fell largely on the backs of the rural population, since the basic taxes were a poll and a land tax, and most other taxes were related to property. These revenues were required either in precious metal or in kind. The precious metal, coin or plate or bullion, was then paid out to the army and civil servants. The feeding of these servants of the State was an immense logistical task, since whereas pay-days only came at intervals, grain, meat, vegetables and other food and drink had to be on the mess tables every day. Taxation in kind raised much of this, and compulsory transport as a form of tax liability ensured part at least of the transport. Even so, the State could not raise enough in taxation to satisfy its needs for goods. Therefore, it arranged to buy in more produce for money, the system of *coemptio*. This was probably an important channel by which taxpayers could obtain coin for paying in precious metals.

In Britain, the standing army had shrunk considerably from its second-century peak of about 50,000 to something probably nearer 15,000 (James 1984). But there is also evidence that the island was regularly called upon to furnish supplies to the army of the Rhine. In the 350s the Caesar Julian restarted exports of grain from Britain to the Rhine and restored the ships and installations. This makes it sound as though there had been a regular movement of supplies earlier (Ammianus Marcellinus XVIII, 2, 3; Julian, Epistle to the Athenians 280 A, C). The increased supervision of the diocese by the civil and financial arms of the imperial government is clear from the lists of officials contained in the *Notitia Dignitatum*.

As well as the demands of the distant but powerful Emperor through his officers and officials on the spot, there were nearer to home the aristocrats and landowners. The Emperor himself undoubtedly owned land in Britain from which he derived income. So also, probably, did wealthy senatorial families based in Rome and Italy. A glimpse of this is offered us in the Life of Saint Melania the Younger in which Britain is mentioned as an area in which her great family held property. The aristocracies of the *civitates* of Britain were a *rentier* class, who derived income and status alike from their estates. Moreover, they were deeply imbued with Roman cultural values, which demanded that much income had to be expended upon residences, displays and pursuits appropriate to their status. Whereas in the second century this had often taken the form of public buildings and benefactions, by the fourth century the emphasis was more on private ostentation and patronage at their residences. This must account for many of the 'town houses' and villas with their reception rooms, mosaics and other fitments which attest to the wealth and taste of this class over southern and eastern Britain. And it was not just buildings and their adjuncts; movables also could be of the most lavish nature as it attested by the contents of some of the hoards of precious objects from late Roman Britain (Painter 1977; Johns and Potter 1983).

There were other specialists in society besides the soldiers who guarded and guaranteed the *status quo*. There were urban artisans and professionals who supplied the needs of the local landowning classes and of the countryfolk. There were the religious specialists such as pagan priests and Christian clergy and bishops, most of whom probably depended on land for their income and sustenance.

The impact of this on the landscape and on the peasantry who had to farm it is not difficult to visualize. There were several levels of demand. There was the taxation system. There was *coemptio*. There were rent and other exactions from landlords to keep themselves in the style to which they were accustomed. There were the townspeople to be fed and the raw materials for their crafts supplied. In the face of such pressure to produce surplus, the farmer can either extensify or intensify, or do both. That is, he can extend the amount of land under cultivation, to the extent of taking into use land previously too marginal to be worthwhile. Or he can use more intensively the land already cleared for use. From late Roman Britain there is evidence for both, as in the appearance of fields on steep slopes and other marginal land, or in the spread of arable onto what had hitherto been pasture in the Thames valley (cf. Esmonde Cleary 1989, pp. 100–16). The evidence from the landscape of late Roman Britain is that it was under considerable pressure to produce surpluses to support the army, the bureaucracy, the aristocracy, the townsfolk and others.

Quite suddenly, in the early fifth century, this stopped. The Roman Empire let Britain slip from its grasp, and the superstructure of State demands and the revenue and payment cycle came crashing down. The effects of this on the economy and material culture of Roman Britain were sudden and catastrophic (Esmonde Cleary 1989, Ch. 4). The surplus extraction which had made possible the distinctive archaeology of late Roman Britain ceased. Indeed we can now appreciate that when we talk of the end of Roman Britain, we are essentially commenting on an archaeological phenomenon: the sudden disappearance of a Roman-style material culture. But material culture is a reflection of social formations and practices, so these must have been suffering in proportion to the loss of their material expression. Not only the imperial level of demand and expenditure was lost, but the evidence is that the more local aristocratic structures cease to be recognizable.

This accords with what we have already noted about British society by the mid to later fifth century. What evidence we have points to a localized, economically underdeveloped society with little evidence for hierarchy or specialization. There is little evidence for surplus extraction, and this may in part have been because there was little to spend it on. It is possible that society now operated in ways that leave little archaeological trace, but as always it is difficult to argue from silence. The small amount of evidence we have for the landscape at this period, for instance from the Thames valley, is that the intensive use of the late Roman period stopped but that the land remained open, though now used in different ways. In sum, the evidence for social hierarchy, specialization and for modes of display in this period is practically nil. Thus the archaeological record has changed, but for reasons to do with society rather than landscape.

Similar points can be made about the areas of England in which the Anglo-Saxons were settling in the mid to late fifth century. Clearly there must have been some level of surplus extraction to 'pay' for the precious metals and craftsmanship evident in many of the objects which people took to the grave with them. But as noted earlier, the evidence from settlements and cemeteries is that the hierarchy was relatively flat and undifferentiated and there is little evidence for specialization outside a domestic/craft level. The evidence from the settlements is for an agrarian, peasant society based on the family and kin. There was status and specialization within this social formation, but apparently little at a regional or wider level. Again, a fairly low level of surplus extraction would have been sufficient for its needs.

It is only in the sixth century that the picture changes again. Archaeologically there start to appear settlements which can be described as 'high status', such as Cowdery's Down, Hampshire (Millett and James 1983). The evidence of the cemeteries is for deepening hierarchy and for increasing differentiation by age, gender and status. In Kent in particular and in other parts of the south-east there start to appear 'royal' or 'princely' burials and cemeteries, marked out from the rest by the more lavish provision of grave-goods in terms of both quantity and quality. This was to culminate in the great cemetery at Sutton Hoo. The range, value and sophistication of the objects in these cemeteries also increases as the century draws on. It is also in the later sixth and early seventh centuries that we can see the processes of state-formation and of the development of kingship at work (Bassett 1989). It is noticeable that one of the prerogatives of a king is the food-render. Clearly the conditions for increasing surplus extraction were developing. There was the process of territorial amalgamation and social development which led to kings and kingdoms appearing. This meant the need to display wealth, to give gifts and reward service. Moreover, there was now more to spend surplus on, as the quality and quantity of grave-goods shows. This was particularly so in Kent, where the influence from Merovingian Gaul was at its strongest.

From Merovingian Gaul also came the other great spur to development. The mission of St Augustine and the gradual conversion of the English (re)introduced to England a very Roman institution, the Church. Though it preached of the world to come, it had a sharp eye for advantage in this world. It was also an institution with its roots and organization in the urban world of the Roman Mediterranean. Its appearance in England gave the new kings and kingdoms a whole new theatre for gift-giving, building and patronage. Surplus and its extraction become a central concern of secular and ecclesiastical authorities throughout the rest of the Anglo-Saxon period and beyond.

I have tried to argue that the idea that the fall of Roman Britain produced a cataclysm in the landscape was based on a misreading of the evidence. As evidence for the basic elements of the landscape—that is its natural constituents and conditions, the crops and herds, the fields and pasture—builds up, it seems more and more likely that there was not cataclysm but changes of emphasis. These were closely tied to a human constraint: the need and ability to extract surplus. This in its turn was a reflection not of the state of the landscape, but of the state of society, of the economy and culture. What changed over these two centuries was not the land, but the culture and habits of the people who lived off it. By distinguishing more clearly between these elements of the landscape we can, as promised at the beginning, come up with a more rounded and, I hope, more interesting picture.

This essay has necessarily, for reasons of space, been written with broad brush strokes. To the individual worker on a site or on a survey it may all seem a bit removed from their concerns. But I hope I have shown and that they will appreciate that the response of a landscape is not only to its local characteristics and its local population, but also to the wider demands made upon it by the culture of which that population is inextricably a part.

References

Bassett, S.R., 1985. 'Beyond the edge of excavation: the topographical context of Goltho', in *Studies in Medieval History Presented to R.H.C. Davis*, ed. H. Mayr-Harting and R.I. Moore (London), pp. 21–39.

Bassett, S.R., (ed.), 1989. *The Origins of Anglo-Saxon Kingdoms* (Leicester).

Bassett, S.R., 1990. 'The Roman and medieval landscape of Wroxeter', in *From Roman Viroconium to Medieval Wroxeter*, ed. P.A. Barker (Worcester), pp. 10–12.

Bassett, S.R., 1992. 'Church and diocese in the West Midlands: the transition from British to Anglo-Saxon control', in *Pastoral Care Before the Parish*, ed. J. Blair and R. Sharpe (Leicester), pp. 13–40.

Bell, M., 1989. 'Environmental archaeology as an index to continuity and change in the medieval landscape', in *The Rural Settlements of Medieval England*, ed. M. Aston, D. Austin and C.C. Dyer (Oxford), pp. 269–86.

Crabtree, P.J., 1991. *West Stow, Suffolk: Early Anglo-Saxon Animal Husbandry*, East Anglian Archaeology 47 (Ipswich).

Davies, W., 1982. *Wales in the Early Middle Ages* (Leicester).

Esmonde Cleary, A.S., 1989. *The Ending of Roman Britain* (London).

Esmonde Cleary, A.S., 1992. 'Town and country in Roman Britain?' in *Death in Towns*, ed. S.R. Bassett (Leicester), pp. 28–42.

Gelling, M., 1984. *Place-Names in the Landscape* (London).

Gildas, *De Excidio Britunum, The Ruin of Britain*, ed. and trans. M. Winterbottom, Arthurian Sources 7 (Chichester, 1978).

Grant, A., 1989. 'Animals in Roman Britain', in *Research on Roman Britain 1960–89*, ed. M. Todd (London), pp. 135–46.

Hamerow, H., 1991. *Excavations at Mucking Volume 2: The Anglo-Saxon Settlement* (London).

Härke, H., 1990. '"Warrior Graves"? The backgound of the Anglo-Saxon weapon burial rite', *Past and Present*, 126, pp. 22–43.

Hoskins, W.G., 1955. *The Making of the English Landscape* (London).

James, H., 1992. 'Early medieval cemeteries in Wales', in *The Early Church in Wales and the West*, ed. N. Edwards and A. Lane (Oxford), pp. 90–103.

James S., 1984. 'Britain and the late Roman army', in *Military and Civilian in Roman Britain*, ed. T.F.C. Blagg and A. King, Br Archaeol Rep, Br Ser, 136 (Oxford), pp. 161–86.

James, S., Marshall, A. and Millett, M., 1984. 'An early medieval building tradition', *Archaeological Journal*, 141, pp. 182–215.

Johns, C. and Potter, T., 1983. *The Thetford Treasure: Roman Jewellery and Silver* (London).
Jones, M., 1981. 'The development of crop husbandry', in *The Environment of Man: the Iron Age to the Anglo-Saxon Period*, ed. M. Jones and G. Dimbleby, Br Archaeol Rep, Br ser, 87 (Oxford), pp. 95–127.
Jones, M., 1989. 'Agriculture in Roman Britain: the dynamics of change', in *Research on Roman Britain 1960–89*, ed. M. Todd (London), pp. 127–34.
Maltby, M., 1981. 'Iron Age, Romano-British and Anglo-Saxon animal husbandry: a review of the evidence', in *The Environment of Man: the Iron Age to the Anglo-Saxon Period*, ed. M. Jones and G. Dimbleby, Br Archaeol Rep, Br ser, 87 (Oxford), pp. 151–203.
Millett, M. and James, S., 1983. 'Excavations at Cowdery's Down, Basingstoke, Hampshire, 1978–81', *Archaeological Journal*, 140, pp. 151–279.
Pader, E-J., 1982. *Symbolism, Social Relations and the Interpretation of Mortuary Remains*, Br Archaeol Rep, Int ser, 130 (Oxford).
Painter, K., 1977. *The Mildenhall Treasure* (London).
Philpott, R., 1991. *Burial Practices in Roman Britain: a survey of grave treatment and furnishing AD 43–410*, Br Archaeol Rep, Br ser, 219 (Oxford).
Rahtz, P., 1977. 'Late Roman cemeteries and beyond', in *Burial in the Roman World*, ed. R.M. Reece, Counc Br Archaeol, Res Rep 22 (London), pp. 53–64.
Sparey Green, C., 1987. *Excavations at Poundbury: Volume I: The Settlements* (Dorchester).
Todd, M., '*Famosa Pestis* and fifth-century Britain', *Britannia*, 8, pp. 319–25.
Turner, J., 1981. 'The vegetation', in *The Environment of Man: the Iron Age to the Anglo-Saxon Period*, ed. M. Jones and G. Dimbleby, Br Archaeol Rep, Br ser, 87 (Oxford), pp. 67–73.
West, S., 1985. *West Stow: the Anglo-Saxon Village*, 2 vols, East Anglian Archaeology 24, (Ipswich).
Williamson, T.M., 1986. 'Parish boundaries and early fields: continuity and discontinuity', *Journal of Historical Geography*, 12 iii, pp. 242–48.
Williamson, T.M., 1987. 'Early co-axial field systems on the East Anglian boulder clays', *Proceedings of the Prehistoric Society*, 53, pp. 419–31.

CHAPTER TWO

Bishoprics, Monasteries and the Landscape, *c.* AD 600–1066

Christopher Holdsworth

The main question to be addressed in this chapter is how did some of the main institutions of Christianity affect the development of the landscape? The distribution of known churches and chapels indicates one part of an answer to this general question: the new faith needed special cult buildings all over the countryside, though whether it actually had them for the whole of the long period with which we are concerned one may doubt. In some areas evidence for such buildings is very rare for most of the period (e.g. Higham 1986, pp. 280–81). But even so it may be useful to offer a reminder at the start as to why such special facilities were needed.

The Christian religion which began to spread, or, perhaps more accurately, to take new roots in England around the end of the sixth century, centred upon the practice of a particular kind of worship. Regularly, week by week, and in some places every day, a ritual meal was shared, accompanied by prayers and readings, sometimes sung, from texts believed to be holy. More irregularly, at the crisis points in the lives of individual members of the worshipping group, special prayers and actions were offered to bless birth, marriage and death. Long before these practices were reintroduced here by missionaries from, on the one hand, the Mediterranean world and, on the other, North Britain, Christians had come to hold that both types of ceremony could best be offered indoors, in a specially set-aside building. Such a development was not inevitable: after all, the founder of the religion had prayed with his followers out of doors or in a borrowed room, and from time to time outdoor areas, or indoor spaces not exclusively dedicated to Christian use, were employed; but Christians rarely gathered for their cult under the stars, still less in sacred groves, or by a numinous seashore. The worship of the Italian monk Augustine, or indeed that of Patrick and Gildas, normally took place indoors in a space consecrated, set aside, for this purpose, though from time to time that space could be used for other public purposes like the holding of a legal court. Preaching and teaching could take place outdoors, sometimes beside a large cross, where a travelling priest, like Cuthbert in Northumbria, could set up his portable altar, perhaps on a pile of stones or table brought from a nearby house, to offer the sacred meal (Mayr-Harting 1972, pp. 247–48; Campbell 1982, pp. 80–81). But the hope of those who brought the faith was to have their own buildings, and those they got, in time, even though most of them are not recoverable by us now.

The preference for buildings exclusively used for their purposes, rather than shared with others, may well be connected with the development of a separate class of clergy, people who depended for their livelihood on their cultic functions rather than on the practice of a craft or trade. The church of New Testament times had been rather different. Records concerning Paul show that he worked as a tent-maker so as not to be a charge on his co-religionists (Acts xviii. 1–3: I Cor. ix. 3–18), and that there were many different kinds of service or ministry within the church, but by our period these had become fewer, more restricted, so that those who professed Christianity, the people, were directed by a smaller section of clergy (Chadwick 1967, pp. 45–53). And half of the human race, those who were female, were left very firmly on the people side of the division except for a small number of abbesses—leaders of communities of women who had renounced normal life for prayer and ascetic practice. One could suggest many explanations for these developments and also suppose that if Christianity had not taken the turning towards a full-time, male-dominated clergy, it might never have needed specialized buildings, but we can be certain that without these developments the landscape would have looked very different.

Here, two areas will be explored: first, the effects of the needs of the highest status clergy, namely bishops, upon the landscape, particularly that of towns; and second, the effects of the needs of those Christians who had adopted a particular form of Christian life, namely that of full-time religious, as monks or nuns, upon the landscape, both urban and rural. Inevitably in one short essay discussion must be rather general, but it is hoped that some maps and diagrams will help to make it accessible.

By the time missionaries brought Christianity to the Anglo-Saxons, the community of faith was led by a small group of specially blessed men called bishops (Chadwick 1967, pp. 46–48, 163–66). Their two main functions were to see that the faith was taught correctly to unbelievers and to the converted, and to ensure that there was a supply of properly trained priests to serve the local communities. Bishops selected and ordained those intended to be priests. In the Italy from which the first missionaries came, there were many bishops in comparison with some other parts of the Christian world, and they generally had their *sedes*, seats, in churches within towns, and the area over which they exercised their authority was the countryside around the town, which also looked to it for certain non-religious services like marketing and the provision of justice. It was not surprising, therefore, that when Pope Gregory, who had initiated the mission to England, instructed Augustine to provide bishops for the new Christians, both of them should have looked for places which appeared as similar as possible to the towns of Italy. Gregory envisaged dividing England into two provinces, each under an archbishop, and expected that Augustine would establish his own base in London, which the Pope called a *civitas*, 'city', like York, which was designed as the centre for the northern province (Bede, *Ecclesiastical History*, I.29: Colgrave and Mynors 1969, pp. 104–6). Perhaps these two places were still known in Rome as centres of the Empire, which by 600 had long lost control of most of its old territory in western Europe, or perhaps someone in the Pope's household had heard of their size and economic significance through Frankish or Flemish traders who had been in England. It is not easy to know why Gregory thought that each province should contain twelve bishops, for anything like that pattern was not achieved in the north for many centuries, but in the south it came into being by AD 737, 140 years after Augustine's arrival (Hill 1981, p. 147). It provided all the major groupings of people in England with their own bishop. Figure 2.1 and Table 2.1 show the sees in both north and south at that time.

Table 2.1 Places with bishops *c.*737 and *c.*1035

Bishoprics	
c.737	*c.1035*
Canterbury R	Canterbury
	Crediton cum St Germans
	Dorchester
Dunwich R	
	Durham
Elmham	Elmham
Hereford	Hereford
Hexham	
Leicester R	
Lichfield	Lichfield
Lindisfarne	
Lindsey R	
London R	London
	Ramsbury
Rochester R	Rochester
Selsey	Selsey
Sherborne	Sherborne
	Wells
Winchester R	Winchester
Worcester R	Worcester
York R	York

The table is based on Figs 2.1 and 2.2, supplemented with information in Morris 1989, p. 9 on Roman places (=R). The West Saxons first had their bishopric at Dorchester R; it moved to Winchester in *c.*663.

The first major question to be faced is what considerations led to these particular places being selected as the centres of dioceses? It is likely that the missionaries were attracted to places which bore some resemblance to familiar Italian ones. Nine of the fifteen locations were indeed places where there had been towns during the Roman period, but so far signs that real urban life had

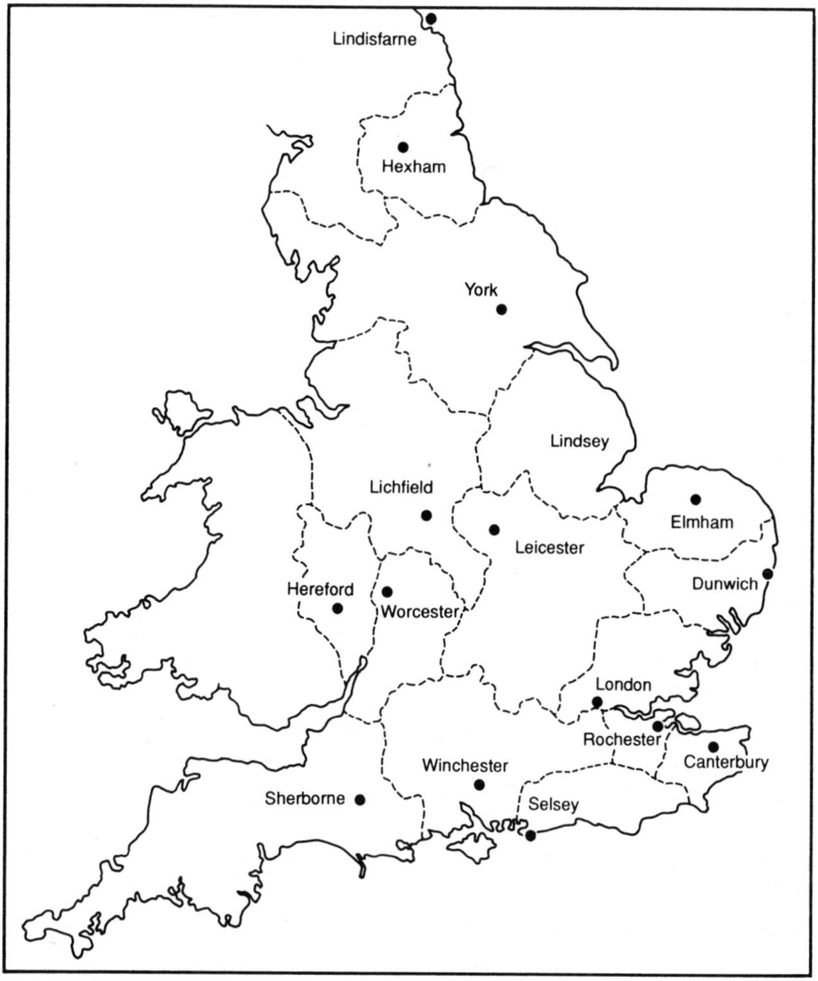

Fig. 2.1 Dioceses AD 850 (after Hill 1981, 238).

continued in them from Roman times is very sparse (Morris 1989, pp. 9, 179–81). York may be the only place which is a clear exception. Recent excavations suggest that the legionary fortress at its centre was still in repair, and presumably in use for some purpose, in the late seventh century (Campbell 1979, pp. 119–20). One may note that even if a Christian community clung on within the old walls of Exeter, for instance, and buried its dead in or around its church (in contrast to the Romans who generally had their cemeteries outwith the city walls), there are few other signs of families making their livelihood from trading and craftwork rather than from agriculture (Allen et al. 1984, pp. 386–89). Canterbury, where Augustine went soon after his arrival in England, was in some sense the political centre of the rule of the king of Kent, yet the archaeological evidence does not, so far, suggest a flourishing urban environment there either (Tatton-Brown 1984, p. 5). And King Æthelberht and his companions may not have been there all that often anyway, since kings then, and indeed for a long time to come, generally went round their kingdoms 'eating up' the produce of their estates. But, nonetheless, at these three places, and at the other Roman sites, it is likely that old walls provided some protection for a bishop and his clergy, against inclement weather as well as the raiding which was a feature of the political life of the time. The old sites were well chosen too in relation to the availability of water, and to communication by land or water. The reasons which had led Romans to choose them still held good. Indeed, other local rulers beside Æthelberht seem to have been drawn to these old towns for similar reasons as the priests. Worcester, for example, was called in a charter dating between AD 718 and 745 the 'metropolis of the Hwicce'. Here, one may also note that a larger old Roman town in the area, Gloucester, did not become the centre of a bishopric, perhaps because a monastery had been established there fairly early, using up a good deal of local resources (Sims-Williams 1990, pp. 89–90). It is scarcely surprising that bishops went to centres of royal power, which were obviously places where kings would have land to give away, since, as far as we can see, the faith spread from the top downwards in Anglo-Saxon society: the ruler's conversion was necessary before the new faith could take root (Campbell 1982, pp. 45–68). And without royal support, how were these men who needed income and buildings to receive the wherewithall to live?

Once a bishop had settled in a town, it is obvious that some kind of community would grow up around him, although hard evidence for the process has disappeared. Every bishop gathered a small group of clergy around him which in its turn needed servants, who brought families and more mouths to feed into each cathedral town. The clerical group itself had some peculiar needs which could not be satisfied by local produce. Wine, not beer or mead, was specified for the ritual meal, and since vines grew rarely in England at this time it had to be imported, whilst incense, by then a usual accompaniment to the ritual (and one may suppose a very necessary one, when cleanliness was no longer equated with citizenship, still less with godliness), had to be brought from distant places. Some of the garments which priests wore when they officiated were made of silk, which had to come from the eastern Mediterranean since the raising of silk worms and the production of silk were only practised there. So traders of various sorts are likely to have been drawn to these new Christian centres, whilst the erection of a church, even in wood, called for the skills of craftsmen of various kinds. Bede makes it clear that when stone churches were called for in Northumberland masons and glass-makers had to be brought over from Francia (*Historia Abbatum*, 5.1: Plummer 1896, I. 368; Campbell, 1982, pp. 74–77). Bishops must have stimulated certain kinds of development in the places where they settled, even though some of the later evidence, discussed next, may make one hesitate before claiming that they were crucial in the growth of towns.

The evidence for the siting of sees at around 1035, the end of the reign of Cnut, shows certain changes from the earlier pattern (Fig. 2.2). In the north, where there had been separate sees centred on Hexham and Lindisfarne, there was now one vast see based on Durham. South of the Humber another see stretched as far south as the Thames valley, uniting what had been the sees of Leicester and Lindsey. Here the bishop's seat was at Dorchester, almost at the extreme southern edge of the diocese. To the south and west, where the West Saxons had been served by merely two dioceses, Winchester and Sherborne, division had occurred creating additional sees at Wells, Ramsbury, Crediton and St Germans, these last two being usually held together. These changes had all been triggered off, in rather different ways, by the Vikings, who had

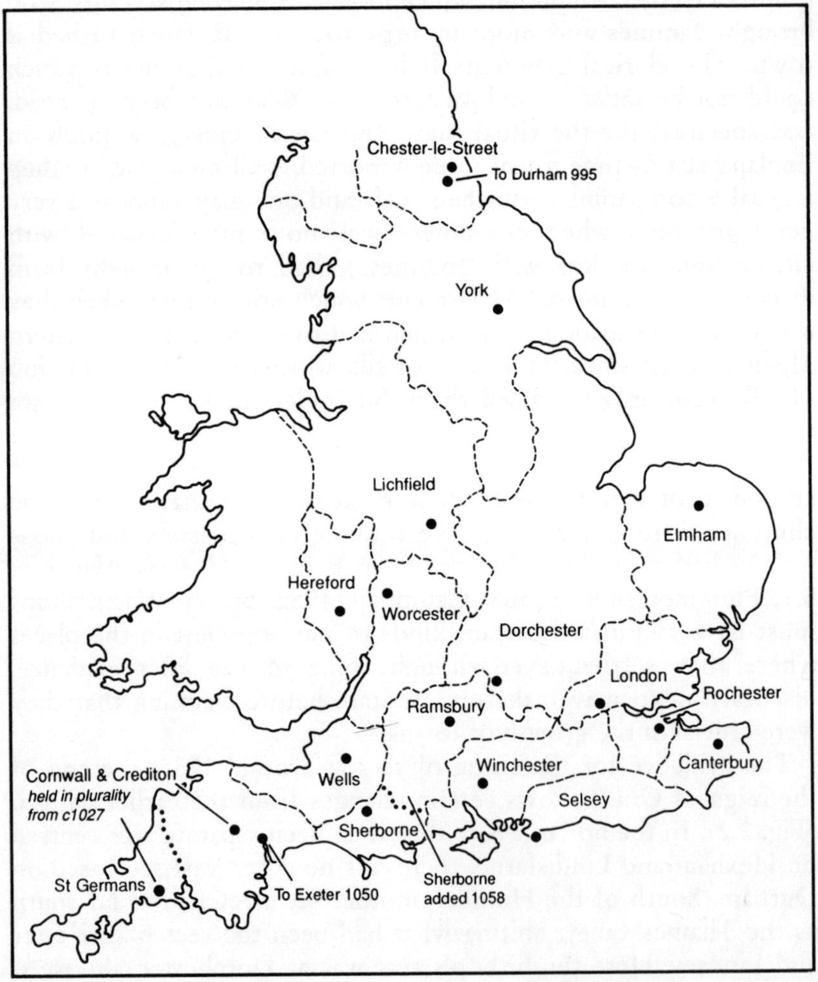

Fig. 2.2 Dioceses AD 1035 (after Hill 1981, 241).

destroyed a number of old centres and also elevated the surviving kingdom of the West Saxons into the most powerful centre of power (Barlow 1979, pp. 162–83, surveys all the dioceses).

It may be asked whether the centres of bishoprics in 1035 were significant places; in particular, were they all sizeable? The answer which seems to be emerging is that some of them were and some of them were not. As is well known, estimates of population largely depend upon Domesday Book, despite the fact that it was not compiled until 1086. This has other drawbacks too. It omits London, the largest town, and because it only records the number of burgage tenements, or burgesses, it may underestimate by perhaps a factor of two or three the number of inhabitants in any one place. Both town-plans and archaeology suggest that there had been considerable division of plots within towns, and consequent 'subletting', even though Domesday itself says nothing about this (Morris 1989, p. 206). So Exeter, for example, with 456 sites, may have had substantially more people so that its population, reckoning five people per household, may be nearer 4,000 than 2,000 (Holdsworth 1986, p. 58; Allen et al. 1984, p. 385).

The whole question of urban size is under much discussion at the moment and another kind of evidence being used is the fairly abundant coinage which survives from the reign of Æthelred II and later, upon which is struck the name of the minter and the town in which he worked. One hypothesis, not accepted by everyone, is that the number of minters producing a particular type of coin gives an indication of the relative economic significance of that centre compared with other centres, and hence of its size (Hill 1981, pp. 126–32; for a different method of ranking see Metcalf 1978 and 1981). Table 2.2 gives towns which had bishops, ranked by the number of mints as a percentage of the total number of moneyers working in the late Anglo-Saxon period. Places which had bishops but lacked moneyers are appended at the bottom of the table. From this it appears that in 1066 ten bishops had their seats in places which did have mints, though some of these places seem to have been fairly small (notably so by this measure were Worcester, Hereford, Rochester and Dorchester) and that there were five bishops in places which lacked even one moneyer in their 'town'. Although any estimate of town size must be fairly speculative, it is striking that only five of the fifteen places with bishops seem to have been in places where there were more than 4,000 or so people. (London, which other evidence suggests had the greatest population, is included among the five.) This may well lead one to suppose that the economic significance of a bishop

Table 2.2 Sites of bishoprics 1066: population and ranking by number of moneyers

Places with bishops with ranking	*Estimated population*
1 London	15–25,000*
[2 Lincoln, 1072]	6,000+*
3 York	8,000+*
4 Winchester	6,000+*
[5 Chester, 1075]	1,500–2,000*
6 Thetford	4–5,000*
7 Exeter	2–4,000
9 Canterbury	3–6,000
[10 Norwich, 1094 × 1096]	6–7,000*
21 Worcester	650–1,300
24 Hereford	1,200–2,400
35 Rochester	575–1,150
56 Dorchester	535
No mints:	
Durham	
Lichfield	270
Selsey	108
Sherborne	965
Wells	475

Three places without bishops in 1066 are included in brackets. Mint ranking is derived from Hill 1981, p. 154, and estimates of population marked * from Morris 1989, p. 178. For Exeter see Holdsworth 1986, p. 58. For the other boroughs I have multiplied the total number of houses and burgesses by five, and indicated a possible maximum to allow for undersettlers and those too poor to be counted after that. For Dorchester, Lichfield, Selsey, Sherborne and Wells, which are not called boroughs in the Domesday Book, I have added together the peasant population and multiplied by five. The results must be very approximate. Durham is not in the Domesday Book.

living in a place may not have been so great as was being suggested earlier. It also makes one ask why bishops stayed in such small places or indeed occasionally, as was the case at Durham, or Wells and Sherborne, moved to them.

The first brake on willingness to move may have been an unwillingness to leave an old hallowed site, a form of conservatism which may have been particularly connected with devotion to some holy Christian hero, less usually a heroine, that is to say a saint (Rollason 1986, 1989). We may note, for example, that by 1035 Worcester had its Oswald, Hereford an Æthelberht (not the king of Kent, but of the East Angles), whilst Rochester had Paulinus, and Lichfield (which lacked even one moneyer) had no less than three old saints, Cedd, Ceadda and Ceata. But an equally powerful restraint in some dioceses was the lack of any considerable alternative site: for example, Worcester and Hereford and Rochester all lacked any realistic alternatives (Hill 1981, pp. 130, 134–42). Other small centres of dioceses like Sherborne and Wells may have attracted bishops because other larger towns like Shaftesbury, in the first case, or Ilchester and Bath, in the second, were not so central to the diocese. One may, however, doubt whether such geographic arguments weighed very heavily in the era before maps and the kind of spatial thinking which they imply existed. The seat for the South Saxons at Selsey, for example, was at the extreme south-western edge of the diocese and when, after the Conquest, the decision was taken to move it to a larger place, the bishop went not to Lewes, which was far more central and had a mint, but to Chichester, which was, like Selsey, at the edge of the diocese. Domesday figures may, indeed, mislead us into thinking that places with very different populations then had possessed such characteristics for a long time. As James Campbell has pointed out in a recent paper, 'Norwich may have been much more like North Elmham in 950 than it had become by 1050' (Campbell 1979, p. 132). And so it is hardly surprising that the bishop was still at North Elmham in 1035. But a quite different consideration probably was decisive: it was not easy to find adequate space within a larger growing town for a cathedral and its associated buildings. We know that later moves made in the twelfth century to Norwich

Table 2.3 Annual revenue in £'s 1086 set against Corbett's classes of secular baronies

	Diocese	*Monastery*
Class A, over £750 (8)	Canterbury 1,750	
	Winchester 1,000	
		Glastonbury 830
		Ely 770
Class B, £400–650 (10)		Christ Church, Cant. 690
		Bury St Edmunds 640
		St Augustine's, Cant. 640
	London 615	
	Dorchester 600	Winchester, Old Minster, 600
	Salisbury 600	
		Westminster 580
	Worcester 480	
		Abingdon 460
	Thetford 420	
Class C, £200–400 (24)		Winchester, New Minster 390
	York 370	
	Exeter 360	Ramsey 360
	Wells 325	
		Peterborough 320
	Hereford 280	
		St Albans 270
		*Shaftesbury 230
	Rochester 220	
	Durham 205	
Class D, £100–200 (36)		Malmesbury 180
		*Barking 160
		Cerne 160
		Coventry 160
		*Romsey 140
	Chichester 138	
		Evesham 130
		Gloucester 100
		St Benet Holme 100
Class D, less than £100		Milton 90
(90–100)	Chester 85	
		Winchcombe 80

See Corbett 1926, pp. 509–10, the numbers in brackets are the lords in each category; Knowles 1963, pp. 702–3: I have rounded his figures to the nearest £10. He gives incomes for 21 other houses. *Houses of nuns.

and Lincoln, from Elmham and Dorchester, needed royal support to clear space where burgesses had been settled for the new buildings (Campbell 1979, pp. 132–33). Overall, we may be left with the unexpected conclusion that the presence of a bishop in a place may not have affected its growth beyond a certain size very much, but on the other hand it may have been decisive in raising some places out of the normal run of villages.

Before leaving bishops and towns, one more thing needs to be underlined: any bishop, his clerical 'family' and their church required considerable economic resources, and on this question Domesday Book provides us with a basis for a comparison between the wealth of bishops and the wealth of lay nobles.

The left-hand side of Table 2.3 lists sees in descending order of wealth as recorded in Domesday, i.e. by their annual income, mainly derived from lands scattered across each diocese. These incomes have been set against the five divisions into which W.J. Corbett divided great secular lords. The conjunction is striking, demonstrating that the leaders of the church had wealth which put them on a level with the very wealthiest men of their day, a strange situation if one recalls the founder of the faith who had pointed out the difficulty of rich men entering into the kingdom which he announced. In the diocese of Exeter (to which the bishop had moved his seat in 1050, perhaps because it had walls and so was safer than Crediton), for example, the bishop drew his income from no less than twenty-four manors in Devon, totalling by one calculation some 77,000 acres, and from another eleven manors in Cornwall: he was the wealthiest man in Devonshire after the king and the sheriff (Holdsworth 1986, p. 52; 1991, pp. 24–25). At Exeter, as in every other town with a bishop, such resources were bringing about the development of a distinct ecclesiastical centre where, around the church which they served, the bishop and his clergy lived. Towns with bishops may not have always been among the largest but they were gaining a special appearance.

The size of the resources syphoned off by bishops from the economy leaves us with a number of questions to which at present there are few answers. Were estates which were held by a bishop likely to be more effectively exploited than those in lay hands?

Elsewhere in this volume Della Hooke remarks that Uffington in Oxfordshire, which belonged to the abbey of Abingdon, was possibly replanned by the abbey (p. 101). Did bishops often do similar economically significant things for their estates? Bearing in mind that they were literate, and so able to read classical agricultural texts, and that their estates usually passed on from one bishop to the next without major dislocations, unlike lay estates where a line might die out or an heir be a minor, one would suspect that on the whole bishops' lands were better managed than other people's. Can we, I wonder, see this in the landscape? Associated with such questions we may wonder whether such estates were more likely to be provided with churches than anyone else's land. Did episcopal manors receive churches sooner than was normal?

The second area of consideration is monasteries, another aspect of the kind of Christianity which Augustine and subsequent Christians practised in England. They were places where some men and women, usually in quite separate communities but occasionally associated together under one head, lived a life mainly spent in corporate and individual prayer, the rest in various forms of work and meditative reading (Chadwick 1967, pp. 174–83; Southern 1970, pp. 214–33). Such centres developed largely because the demands of the new religion were hard to follow in the everyday world, particularly demands relating to violence and sex, so some people withdrew from wider society to seek salvation in a monastery. There, apart from saving themselves, they were also supposed to pray for the salvation of those still in the world, especially for those who had provided the land and income which supported their own monastery. Monks and nuns were the soul-savers of society at large.

The point comes across in the opening words of one of the earliest genuine documents recording a gift to a monastery, a grant by a sub-king of Surrey to a community at Chertsey, which can be dated to AD 672–74:

> In the name of the Lord Saviour Jesus Christ. I, Frithuwold, concede this donation of my right for the liberty of every single thing. How often so ever we devote any thing to the members of Christ as an act of piety, we trust to benefit our soul, because

> we render to him his own property, and do not bestow ours. (Whitelock 1979, p. 479).

The words, echoing Christ's words about rendering to Caesar and to God those things which belong to each (Mark xii. 14–17 and parallels in Matthew and Luke), were popular, being used by draftsmen of charters in two other kingdoms (Whitelock 1979, pp. 484, 487). A few years after Frithuwold, one of the kings of Kent, Hlothhere, in a charter in favour of the abbot of Reculver, used words found in thousands of subsequent charters, conveying the idea that salvation itself comes from such a gift:

> In the name of our Lord and Saviour Jesus Christ, I, Hlothhere, king of the people of Kent, grant for the relief of my soul, land in Thanet which is called *Westan ac* [i.e. west of the river] to you Brithwold and your monastery . . . (Whitelock 1979, p. 482).

Figure 2.3 shows how extremely widespread were these institutions by the ninth century. The map calls them minsters, the English translation of the Latin *monasterium*. The exact status of such places at that time is not clear; many of them may have been what we would now call monasteries, inhabited by men or women who had adopted a celibate, disciplined form of life, but others would have had communities of clerks, clergy, living together as a community but not necessarily following one of the monastic rules (Morris 1989, pp. 93–139; Foot 1990). Together they are certainly thickly scattered across the whole of England when archaeological and literary evidence are both considered (but one may note that so far archaeological evidence alone is still fairly thin).

Three questions occur when faced with this evidence, mostly parallel to those already considered in relation to bishops' sees. What factors affected the placing of these institutions? How costly were they to establish and maintain? And what special facilities did they need?

The siting of monasteries may have been affected from two different angles by the interests of founders and by the desires of the religious themselves. Kings and great lords set up houses where

Fig. 2.3 Early dioceses and minsters to *c.*850.

they themselves had land to give, in a town like Canterbury or Gloucester, for example, or in the countryside. A rural, indeed rather isolated, setting seems to have been preferred by the monks who settled in Northumbria (Morris 1979, pp. 106–11). One may notice, for example, minsters on islands, like Lindisfarne; on promontories overlooking the sea, as at Coldingham, Tynemouth, Hartlepool and Whitby; by the meeting of rivers as at Jarrow; or among the hills, as at Crayke, Hackness, Coxwold and Stonegrave. These last may have suited smaller communities, or even single hermits very well. But some places housed considerable numbers. The two communities of Jarrow and Wearmouth, founded by the same nobleman, contained in Bede's time around 600 monks. Such sites may well have resembled 'towns' more than secular towns did at that time (Campbell 1979, p. 121).

It is obvious that such large groups must have needed considerable resources, and written histories and charters show that they received them. Bede tells us that Jarrow and Monk Wearmouth received enough land for seventy and forty households respectively, a unit of measure which the Old English version of his *Ecclesiastical History* rendered as so many hides (*Historia Abbatum*, i. 4 and 7: Plummer 1896, I. 367, 370; Hunter-Blair 1956, p. 268; Wallace-Hadrill 1988, p. 33, commenting on *Eccles. Hist.* I. 25). If one supposes that the typical family then had five or six members, it can be seen that Bede's community of 600 with their 110 hides was perhaps not living very much better than laymen might have done. Nonetheless a lot of land was involved. If one looks south from Bede's corner, it is easy to find other well-supported, and presumably numerous, communities. Pagham in Sussex, for example, had lands calculated as containing 70 hides, and Abingdon, south of Oxford, 170 (Morris 1989, p. 112, cf. Sims-Williams 1990, pp. 369–70, for monasteries among the Hwicce). On the other hand, one also finds communities with more meagre support. King Oswiu of Northumbria, for example, established twelve communities, to each of which he gave ten hides, which Bede described as *possessiunculi*, 'smallish estates' (*Eccles. Hist.* III 24: Colgrave and Mynors 1969, p. 291; Higham, 1986, p. 282, thinks the term means 'Bede considered these grants rather frugal', but see Wallace-Hadrill 1988, p. 122, for a different view). But even so we may suppose that even they could have supported between fifty and sixty monks each, a far larger number than were in many communities in the far better documented twelfth century (Holdsworth 1991, pp. 38–39, 40–41).

The special facilities needed by monks and nuns were probably very much simpler than those enjoyed by their spiritual descendants five or six hundred years later. Excavations at Jarrow reveal a very modest set of buildings, lacking a church large enough to contain all the monks at any one time (Cramp 1976). Nonetheless some of the earliest and largest stone buildings created by the Anglo-Saxons were designed for minsters: one may cite Brixworth in Northamptonshire as an example (Stafford 1985, pp. 99–100). Their kind of life, fairly similar to that of bishops in this respect, could not be entirely supplied locally; they too needed wine, incense and material for vestments. One of their activities, bookmaking, could only take place if they had many skins from calves or sheep to hand. In Bede's time his community made three great Bibles, each fairly unusually containing the complete text, needing altogether parchment from 1,550 calves (Mayr-Harting 1972, p. 155). It seems likely that they took these from their own large herds, pastured on their own land.

Moving on to examine the situation around 1035, Figure 2.4 shows a rather different pattern of religious communities than that observed in the eighth century. It shows houses which had been founded from 940 onwards, many of them during the reign of Edgar (959–75) (Campbell, 1982, pp. 181–91; Dales 1988; Yorke 1988). New foundations were necessary because the earlier houses had either been destroyed by the Vikings, like Lindisfarne, or transformed into communities of the second, less monastic type mentioned above, as at the Old Minster, Winchester. The map shows clearly that the geographical area affected by the so-called Tenth-Century Reformation was much smaller than the area where monasticism flourished in the eighth century. With the exception of Coquet Island where there was a hermitage, no monastery existed north of the Humber, and only two small and short-lived communities lay north of a line drawn from the Dee estuary to the

Wash, Alkborough and Stow (Knowles and Hadcock 1971, pp. 52, 53, 57). The vast majority of monasteries for men, or women, and there were far fewer of those, lay south and east of the Severn-Wash line.

Why was this, since one might suppose that men must have felt the need for communities of prayer equally intensely wherever they might have lived? The explanation seems to be that these communities, like their predecessors, needed so much land for their support that only kings had enough to give, and the West Saxon kings, who by now ruled most of the area over which many kings had once ruled, had the bulk of their land in the south (Stafford 1985, pp. 128–29). Devon provides us with two

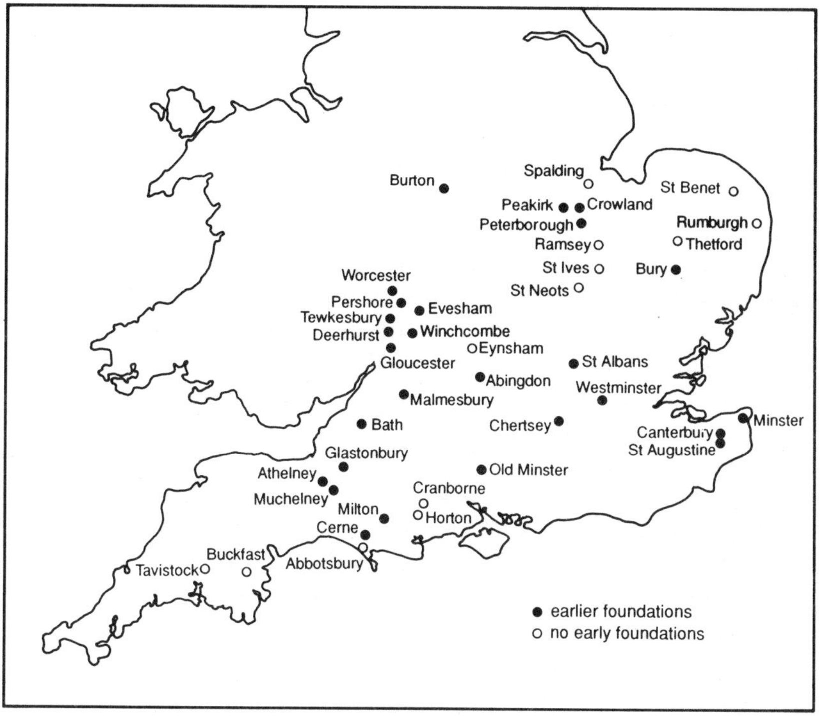

Fig. 2.4 Benedictine Houses (after Hill 1981, 246).

monasteries founded by nobles, Tavistock and Buckfast, but in both cases the founders were men closely connected to the king (Orme 1991, pp. 10, 17). About half these new monasteries were at places where there had been earlier ones, but many were not.

Domesday Book reveals very clearly that some of these monasteries, like most of the bishops, enjoyed large revenues, some of them greater than bishops (Knowles 1963, pp. 702–3). Table 2.3 sets their income against Corbett's five grades of barons. David Knowles calculated that around the time of the Conquest these huge resources were enjoyed by a mere 844 monks and 250 nuns, living in 61 houses in all (Knowles and Hadcock 1971, p. 494), whilst Corbett argued that, when all resources controlled by the Church are added together, around a sixth of the landed wealth of England was involved (Corbett 1926, p. 507; Knowles 1963, pp. 100–3, comes to the same conclusion).

This essay ends with three rather disparate points. Monasteries by the eleventh century were supported by enormous resources, providing them with the potential power to undertake huge building work and to maintain a high lifestyle, provided mainly by the king or the high nobility. No doubt one of their motives was to glorify their God, but one may also suppose that they were also concerned to provide a good setting for their relatives who took on the role of monks or nuns. Most religious did not do this of their own unfettered will but entered the monastic life as children, given by their parents: hence their name of oblate, literally 'someone offered' (Southern 1970, pp. 224, 228–30). Once admitted they may have had few private possessions but could live in high style. Such places, with a certain standard of literacy and continuity of possession, were able (like bishops) to afford to take a long view of the development of their estates and so undertake work which transformed certain parts of the landscape, although we yet do not know whether individual monastic villages, like episcopal ones, were better run than those held by secular lords. Lastly, we may note that the areas where monasticism had been replanted by 1066, in which probably the main economic surplus had been mopped up, largely determined where new houses could be founded in the two hundred years after 1066. Then it was generally on poorer, more marginal land where monks could be given a start, and fortunately for some of these monks at least, this was the sort of land which they said they preferred to have, since it would isolate them from the world all the better (Southern 1970, pp. 250–55).

There can be no doubt that the needs of bishops and monks for support attracted huge resources. We have seen that this was true in the eighth century and in the eleventh. The men and women who provided them were, one must suppose, convinced that such a diversion of wealth was entirely necessary. As a result, every part of the countryside in which they lived had been profoundly affected, even though much of the detailed story of these changes still remains to be traced and described.

References

Allen, J., Henderson, C. and Higham, R., 1984. 'Saxon Exeter', in *Anglo-Saxon Towns in Southern England*, ed. J. Haslam (Chichester) pp. 385–411.

Barlow, F., 1979. *The English Church 1000–1066* (London).

Campbell, J. 1979. 'The Church in Anglo-Saxon towns', in *The Church in Town and Countryside*, ed. Derek Baker, Studies in Church History 16 (Oxford), pp. 119–35: reprinted, Campbell, J., *Essays in Anglo-Saxon History* (London 1986), pp. 139–54.

Campbell, J. (ed.), 1982. *The Anglo-Saxons* (Oxford).

Chadwick, H., 1967. *The Early Church* (Harmondsworth).

Colgrave, B. and Mynors, R.A.B., 1969. *Bede's Ecclesiastical History of the English People* (Oxford).

Corbett, W.J., 1926. 'The development of the duchy of Normandy and the Norman Conquest of England', in *Cambridge Medieval History*, ed. H.M. Gwatkin, J.P. Whitney, J.R. Tanner, C.W. Prévité-Orton and Z.N. Brooke (Cambridge) 5, pp. 505–13.

Cramp, R., 1976. 'Monkwearmouth and Jarrow: the archaeological evidence', in *Famulus Christi: essays in commemoration of the thirteenth centenary of the birth of Bede the Venerable*, ed. G. Bonner (London), pp. 5–18.

Dales, D., 1988. *Dunstan Saint and Statesman* (Cambridge).

Foot, S., 1990. 'What was an early Anglo-Saxon monastery', in *Monastic Studies The Continuity of Tradition*, ed. J. Loades (Bangor), pp. 48–57.

Haslam, J. (ed.), 1984. *Anglo-Saxon Towns in Southern England* (Chichester).
Higham, N., 1986. *The Northern Counties to AD 1000* (London).
Hill, D., 1981. *An Atlas of Anglo-Saxon England* (Oxford).
Holdsworth, C., 1986. 'The Church at Domesday', in *Domesday Essays*, ed. C. Holdsworth, Exeter Studies in History 14 (Exeter), pp. 51–64.
Holdsworth, C., 1991. 'From 1050 to 1307', in *Unity and Variety: A History of the Church in Devon and Cornwall*, ed. N. Orme, Exeter Studies in History 29 (Exeter), pp. 23–50.
Hunter-Blair, P., 1956. *An Introduction to Anglo-Saxon England* (Cambridge).
Knowles, D., 1963. *The Monastic Order in England*, 2nd edn (Cambridge).
Knowles, D. and Hadcock, R.N., 1971. *Medieval Religious Houses England and Wales*, 2nd edn (London).
Mayr-Harting, H., 1972. *The Coming of Christianity to Anglo-Saxon England* (London).
Metcalf, D.M., 1978. 'The ranking of boroughs: numismatic evidence for the reign of Ethelred II', in *Ethelred the Unready*, ed. D. Hill, Br Archaeol Rep, Br Ser, 59 (Oxford), pp. 159–212.
Metcalf, D.M., 1981. 'Continuity and change in English monetary history *c.*973–1086', *British Numismatic Journal*, 51, pp. 73–78.
Morris, R., 1989. *Churches in the Landscape* (London).
Orme, N., 1991. 'From the beginnings to 1050', in *Unity and Variety: A History of the Church in Devon and Cornwall*, ed. N. Orme, Exeter Studies in History 29 (Exeter), pp. 1–22.
Plummer, C. (ed.), 1896. *Venerabilis Baedae Opera Historica*, 2 vols (Oxford).
Rollason, D., 1986. 'The shrines of saints in later Anglo-Saxon England', in *The Anglo-Saxon Church: Papers on History, Architecture and Archaeology in Honour of Dr H.M. Taylor*, ed. L.A.S. Butler and R.K. Morris, Counc Br Archaeol, Res Rep 60 (London), pp. 32–43.
Rollason, D., 1989. *Saints and Relics in Anglo-Saxon England* (Oxford).
Sims-Williams, P., 1990. *Religion and Literature in Western England 600–800* (Cambridge).
Southern, R.W., 1970. *Western Society and the Church in the Middle Ages* (Harmondsworth).
Stafford, P., 1985. *The East Midlands in the Early Middle Ages* (Leicester).
Tatton-Brown, T., 1984. 'The towns of Kent' in *Anglo-Saxon Towns in Southern England*, ed. J. Haslam (Chichester), pp. 1–36.

Wallace-Hadrill, J.M., 1988. *Bede's Ecclesiastical History of the English People A Historical Commentary* (Oxford).

Whitelock, D., 1979. *English Historical Documents c.500–1042*, 2nd edn. (London).

Wormald, P., 1982. 'The age of Bede and Aethelbald', in *The Anglo-Saxons*, ed. J. Campbell (London), pp. 70–100.

Yorke, B. (ed.), 1988 *Bishop Aethelwold His Career and Influence* (Woodbridge).

CHAPTER THREE

Changes in the Cornish Countryside AD 400–1100

Peter Rose and Ann Preston-Jones

The lack of Romanization in Cornwall and the belated conquest by Wessex should lead us to expect a high degree of continuity in the countryside. We are fortunate in that there is an abundance of evidence concerning the settlements at either end of this period, although the character of this evidence is quite diverse. At the beginning of the period our picture is drawn entirely from archaeology, in particular from the abundance of deserted Romano-British enclosed settlements, known in Cornwall as 'rounds', but also from the rich archaeological landscapes of West Penwith, where the settlements of Romano-British courtyard houses are found in the context of the field systems that supported them. At the other end of the period we have exceptionally valuable information from place-names but very little archaeological evidence.

In this chapter we are concentrating on a particular aspect of the countryside, namely patterns of settlement. We shall briefly consider the character of settlements and settlement patterns at each end of this period and then use some local examples to investigate the relationship between them. In outline, the framework we are proposing is that in many essentials the character and distribution of settlement remained very similar, but also that there was dislocation in, say, the fifth and sixth centuries which saw some retraction in the extent and density of settlement; this is likely to have been accompanied both by social change and some change in the settlement type.

The evidence for early medieval settlement in Cornwall has recently been summarized (Preston-Jones and Rose 1986). Assuming the places recorded in medieval documents and having habitative place-name elements of early medieval origin (e.g. *tre*, **bod*[1]: Padel 1985, pp. 24, 223–27) actually represent the locations of early medieval settlements (and there is little reason to doubt this), then it is possible to reconstruct very fully the pattern of early medieval settlement in Cornwall, both generally and in more detail parish by parish (Preston-Jones and Rose 1986, Figs 3, 4 and 5). Places with Cornish topographic names can be less certainly identified as early *settlements*, but since many are recorded in Domesday Book, and their distribution generally meshes with the habitative names, it is likely that a high proportion represent early medieval settlements. The typical pattern is of dispersed settlements spaced at intervals of mostly between 600 and 1,000 m along the valley sides. In lowland Cornwall this gives the impression of an almost continuous dense scatter of settlements, whilst on higher ground the upland areas are fringed and avoided. Even in the lowland areas many ridges and exposed plateaux are likely to have been heath or downland, and often remained so up to the eighteenth or nineteenth centuries. The much larger tracts of heath or moorland across the major granite uplands, including Bodmin Moor and the upland spine of West Penwith, are reflected in the large figures for pasture cited in Domesday Book (Ravenhill 1967, p. 333). These areas would have been a major resource particularly for seasonal grazing (sometimes probably as transhumance) and for the gathering of fuel (Preston-Jones and Rose 1986, pp. 141–44; Herring 1986; Austin et al. 1989; Johnson and Rose 1994).

Compared to most counties Cornwall had relatively little woodland at the time of Domesday Book (Ravenhill 1967, p. 327, Fig. 74; Darby 1967, p. 377, Fig. 89). Interestingly the general pattern of surviving ancient woodland (Nature Conservancy

[1]An asterisk before a word indicates that the item is not recorded, but it is inferred from place-names or other philological evidence.

Council 1986) is broadly similar to that shown by Domesday Book, concentrated in parts of the south and east of the county. We might therefore expect most of our ancient woodlands to be at least a thousand years old. Many other areas of early woodland, for example along the sides of steep valleys, must have been cleared; Pounds notes, for example, that not one of fifteen occurrences of the place-name Pengelly (**pen gelli*, 'grove's end': Padel 1985, p. 180) is nearer than a quarter-mile to a wood, and in most cases there is none within a mile (Pounds 1947, p. 111).

At present only the excavations at Mawgan Porth provide an insight into the character of rural settlements in the tenth to eleventh centuries (Bruce Mitford 1956). This site seems to demonstrate that the characteristic settlement type of the later medieval period, the hamlet of long-houses with ancillary buildings, was already established by this date. It is likely that settlements of the tenth and eleventh centuries, as later, would have been dispersed hamlets and farms.

Study of place-names and topography gives many indications of the expansion of settlement onto higher ground during the early medieval period. Two examples may be mentioned. First, in the parish of North Petherwin in east Cornwall four places with the English element *worðig* seem to represent colonization of the highest ground in the parish, mostly above 150 m (500 ft). Below this is a zone of twelve names with the element *cot*, indicating an earlier phase of colonization into the bleaker parts of the parish (Preston-Jones and Rose 1986, p. 143). On Bodmin Moor the Domesday manors of Hammett and Hamatethy contain the place-name element **havos*, 'shieling'. As Padel points out 'they must therefore represent an expansion of farming settlement, at some time before the late eleventh century, such that what had previously been marginal land became permanent settlements' (1985, p. 127). These indications serve to emphasize the greater antiquity of the 'core' areas of early medieval settlement from which this expansion occurred; on the basis of the linguistic evidence the **tre* place-names could have been coined as early as the sixth century (Padel 1985, pp. 223–24).

If many of Cornwall's farming settlements are of early medieval origin it raises the question of which other elements in the fabric of the countryside are of similar antiquity. Presumably many of the lanes and tracks are as old as the settlements they serve, and the same may apply to the field boundaries. A good example where this is likely is in the Lowland Point area of St Keverne on the Lizard, illustrated by Rackham (1986, p. 162, Fig. 8.5). Another, the Tintagel area, is presented here (Fig. 3.1) to show the problem and the potential.[2] Here and elsewhere in Cornwall much of the pattern seen today reflects the perpetuation of elements of medieval strip field systems (Preston-Jones and Rose 1986, pp. 151–53) but it is likely that at least some of the structure, perhaps much of it, is early medieval in origin. In Figure 3.1 the principal elements in the field patterns, i.e. those abutted by at least three other boundaries, have been selected to suggest what the skeleton of the hypothetical early layout may have looked like. The pattern here is of a succession of extensive irregular rectilinear field systems with settlements scattered throughout. If this pattern is not essentially early medieval then there must have been a major reorganization of the countryside in the later medieval period, which in itself would be a very interesting phenomenon to explore further. Another possibility is that much of the layout is of prehistoric origin; certainly, as noted below, extensive prehistoric rectilinear field systems are known in Cornwall, in West Penwith.

In summary, certainly by the tenth and eleventh centuries, and very probably for centuries before that, we can see a countryside densely occupied with dispersed settlements—quite probably hamlets and single farms—perhaps sitting in extensive rectilinear field systems (at least in some areas). There are indications of a degree of expansion and colonization during the early medieval

[2]In Figs 3.1, 3.3, 3.4 and 3.5 the documented medieval settlements shown are likely to be mostly of early medieval origin; this is particularly so for those with the place-name element *tre* ('farm, estate, hamlet': Padel 1985, pp. 223–27). Also differentiated is the place-name element **ker* ('fort, a round': ibid., pp. 50–54). In these figures earthwork and cropmark enclosures thought to represent Iron Age and Romano–British settlements are denoted as rounds.

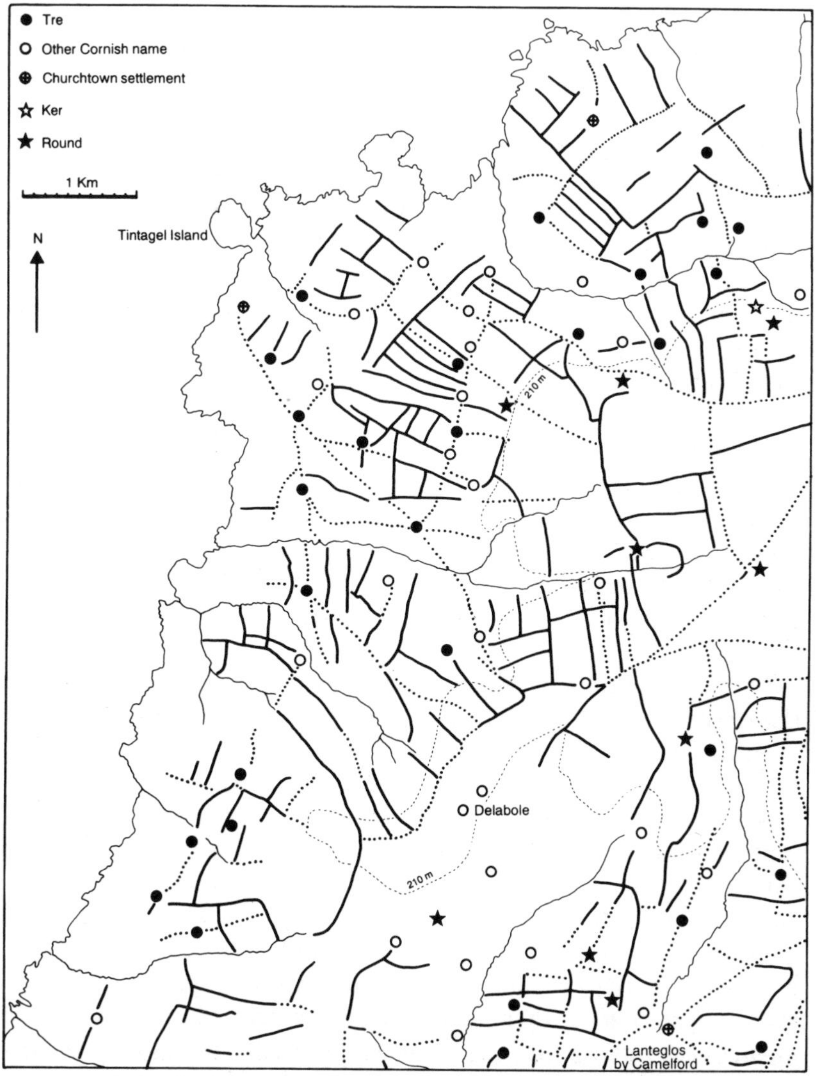

Fig. 3.1 Late prehistoric enclosures and documented medieval settlements in the Tintagel area, showing principal elements in the patterns of fields (solid lines) and trackways (dotted lines). (Centred SX 06 86)

period, but at the same time sizeable areas of heath and moor would have played an important role in the pattern of land use.

Turning to the beginning of the period, enclosed settlements—rounds—are known in hundreds, surviving variously as earthwork enclosures, or perpetuated in modern hedges, or visible as crop-marks or soilmarks (Johnson and Rose 1982). The excavated sites have been dated from perhaps the fourth century BC to the sixth century AD. Best known is Trethurgy, excavated by Henrietta Quinnell in 1973 and still the only totally excavated round (Miles and Miles 1973; Quinnell 1986, pp. 126–27). The sub-circular enclosure, which measured 56 × 48 m internally, was occupied, from the late second century AD to the sixth century, by up to five houses. In Ireland, by way of comparison, the early medieval ring-forts are predominantly small, with an internal diameter generally of only 15–35 m (Edwards 1990, p. 14) and may be regarded as single farmsteads. The Cornish rounds are mostly larger than this and cover a greater range of sizes. Of the large sample illustrated by Johnson and Rose (1982, p. 191, Fig. 3) at least half are the size of Trethurgy or larger and should be regarded, without prejudice to their status and social context, as the equivalent of hamlets. Perhaps only a quarter of the illustrated rounds were single farmsteads.

The distribution of the rounds is broadly similar to that of the early medieval settlements, concentrating on the reasonable farming areas and avoiding the major uplands such as Bodmin Moor, which were presumably used for seasonal grazing (Preston-Jones and Rose 1986, Fig. 3). In some areas, even though our picture is inevitably incomplete, the density and distribution of rounds is not unlike that of the early medieval settlements (Fig. 3.2; Johnson and Rose 1982, p. 204, Fig. 16) with many of the enclosures at intervals of between 500 and 1,000 m. Whilst we can be confident that not all of these sites are contemporary, we can also expect that further sites will be located. These may include *unenclosed* settlements, as in West Penwith (Johnson and Rose 1982, p. 175) but even without such sites the density of settlements is considerable; the impression is of a countryside well populated with enclosed hamlets and farmsteads.

Air photography and geophysical survey is increasingly showing evidence for field systems associated with the enclosures but almost invariably in only tantalizing fragments. As yet we have no clear evidence for the layout, organization and use of these fields. The cropmarks shown in Figure 3.2 provides what is at present our most complete picture of an articulated landscape incorporating rounds and their fields. This is an initial sketch plot compiled from photographs taken in the course of the Cornwall Archaeological Unit's Air Photography Project (directed by Steve Hartgroves and funded by the RCHME) and must be regarded as an interim statement. Nevertheless, it will serve to illustrate some important points. First, we should note the density of settlement, with four enclosures within a square kilometre and each between 400 and 800 m from the next. This is at least as dense as the distribution of early medieval settlements. With such a density it seems less likely that unenclosed settlements were also a major component in the contemporary settlement pattern, at least in this area. Second, we can see something of the settlements' context in an enclosed, farmed countryside; presumably the boundaries comprised a ditch with a bank thrown up on one side, perhaps with a hedge on top. We can also see how the medieval settlement of Trenithan Bennett intrudes into this pattern, with its fields paying no regard to the earlier layout. The impression is that the enclosures and their fields represent a relict landscape, a tract of abandoned countryside, and when the area was subsequently resettled the old field boundaries were not reused in the new field pattern.

This introduces the question of the relationship between the rounds and the early medieval settlements. In Figure 3.3 the enclosures at Trenithan are set in a wider context. In general the rounds seem to fit into the pattern of *medieval* settlement, slotting into gaps in the distribution and extending it into higher ground.

To develop the discussion further we are proposing the following simple model. By the end of the Roman period the countryside was densely occupied with hamlets and farms. This formed the basis of the medieval pattern, with many settlements continuing on more or less the same location, though no longer maintaining their defences. But also in, say, the fifth and sixth centuries, there was a

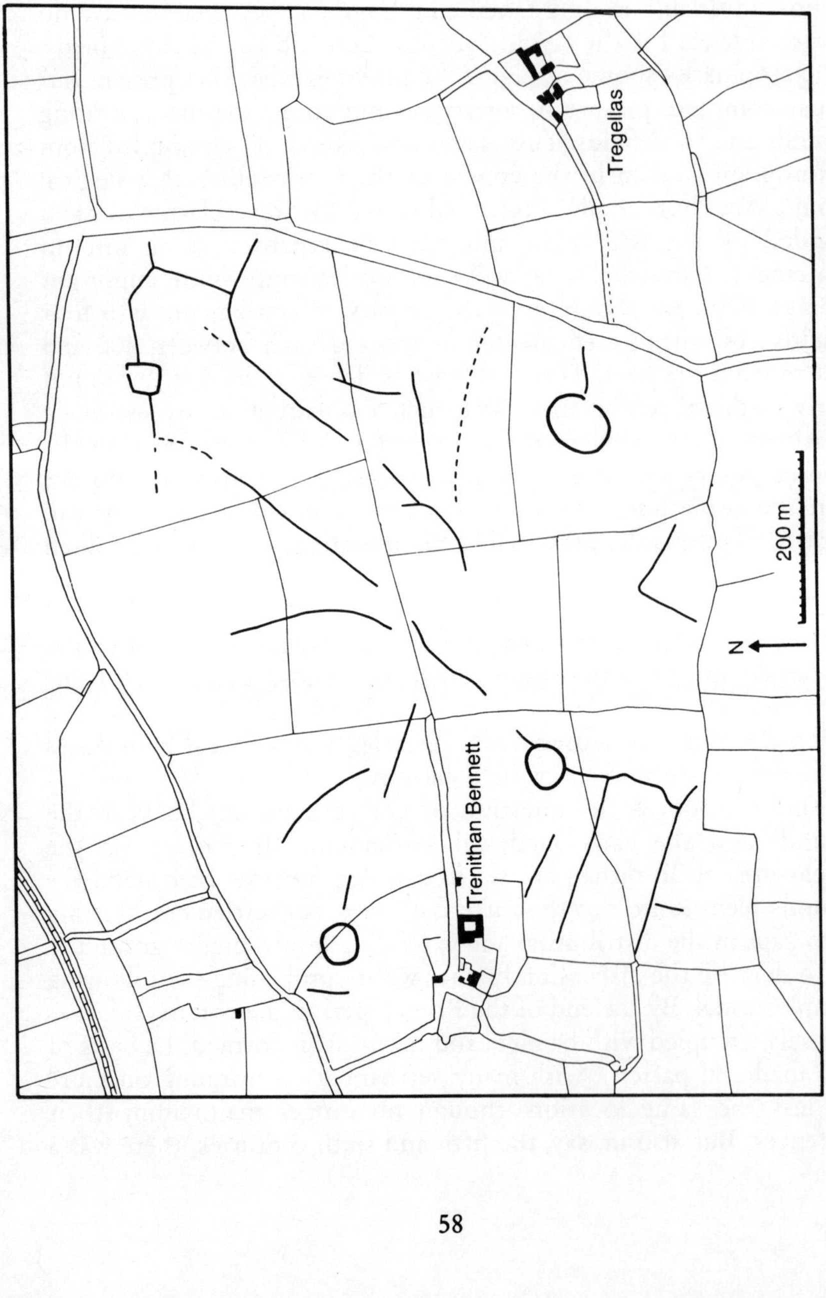

Fig. 3.2 Sketch plot of cropmarks at Trenithan Bennett. (Centred SW 913 493)

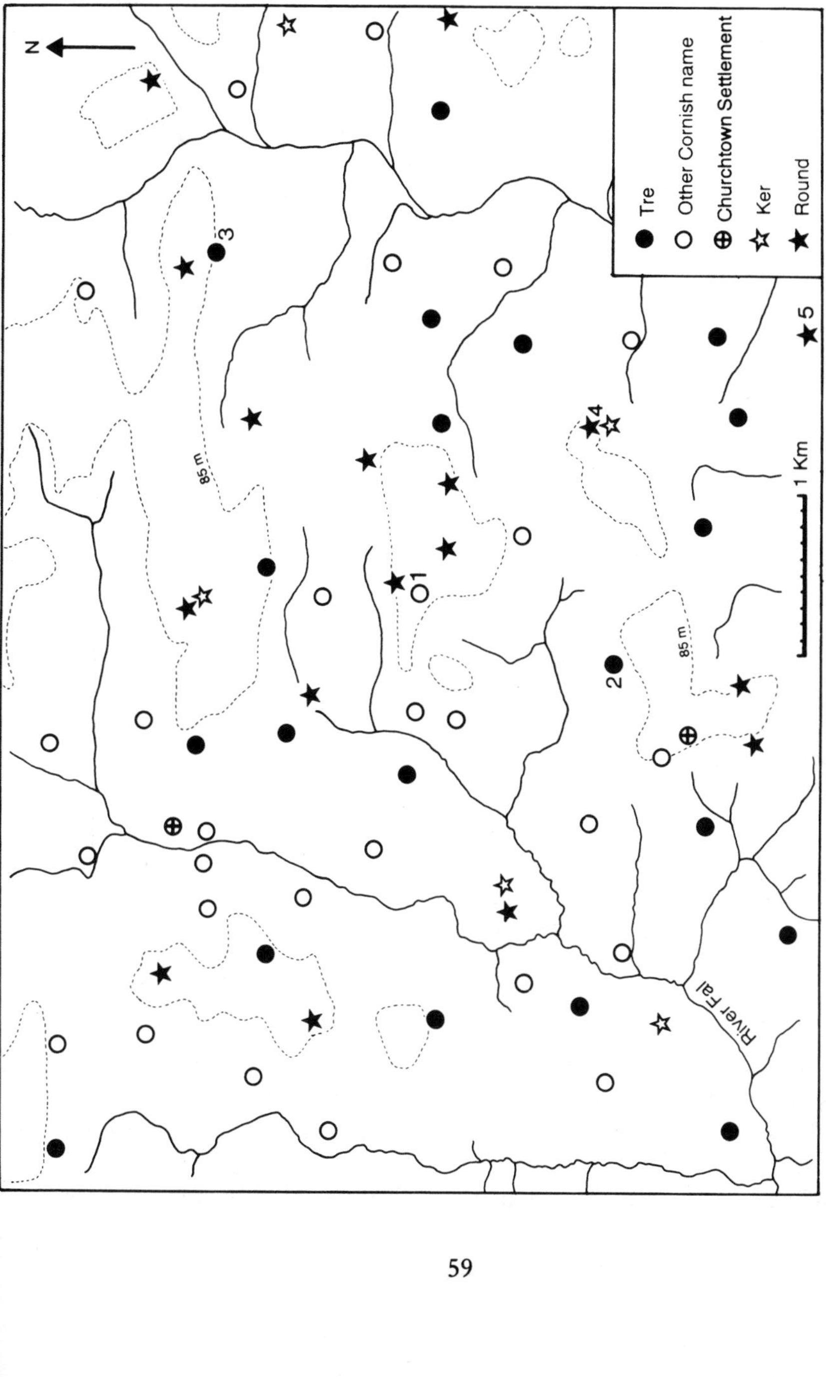

Fig. 3.3 The cropmark enclosures at Trenithan Bennett in the context of medieval and late prehistoric settlements. 1: Trenithan Bennett; 2: Trenithan Chancellor; 3: Trenoweth; 4, 5: major enclosures at Carvossa and Golden. (Centred SW 909 496)

retraction in the extent of settlement, affecting both individual sites within the pattern and sometimes larger areas of countryside. Subsequently—and this may have been at any time over the next few centuries—many of these areas were resettled but not necessarily reusing the same pattern of fields or the same settlement sites.

This may well be the context for the enclosures at Trenithan. They are on a watershed on some of the highest ground in the area, above 85 m (275 ft), and it is likely that much of the high ground to the north-east may also have been depopulated. In this area Trenoweth (No. 3 on Fig. 3.3), 'the new *tref*', is first documented in AD 969 (Padel 1985, p. 225), suggesting reoccupation here by this date. Trenithan Bennett on the other hand may only have been established in the full medieval period, as an offshoot of Trenithan Chancellor to the south (No. 2 on Fig. 3.3).

Figure 3.4 provides a further example. Recent aerial photography in the parishes of Padstow and St Merryn has identified at least twelve enclosures. Significantly, in this relatively low-lying area, the enclosures and medieval settlements are quite similarly located; two enclosures are at the same height as the nearest medieval settlement, five are higher and five are lower. Elsewhere in Cornwall, where there is greater variation in altitude, the rounds are mostly on higher ground; for example, in the ten kilometre square defined by Ordnance Survey grid reference SW 85 almost all the rounds are 8–30 m (25–100 ft) above the nearest medieval settlement (a similar situation is seen in the Tintagel area, see Fig. 3.1). In the light of Figure 3.4 this suggests not that there was a move from higher ground to colonize lower ground at the end of the Roman period, but that the higher settlements were abandoned and the lower settlements continued.

In the framework of our model we can see that some of the enclosures (four of the twelve) fill out the medieval pattern, whilst others (five) are relatively close to medieval settlements (within 200–300 m) and may represent a slight shift in the position of the settlement, or desertion followed by reoccupation in another location.

Work in Somerset has identified a clearer relationship between the medieval and Romano-British settlements; the deserted Romano-British settlements fit into gaps in the spacing of the medieval settlement pattern in a non-random manner, such that the Romano-British and medieval settlements appear to belong to the same pattern of settlement; the medieval settlements, it is suggested, were of Romano-British origin (Leech 1982). Compared to this the situation in Cornwall seems more complex, so that the relationship seen in Figure 3.4 appears random and could indeed be

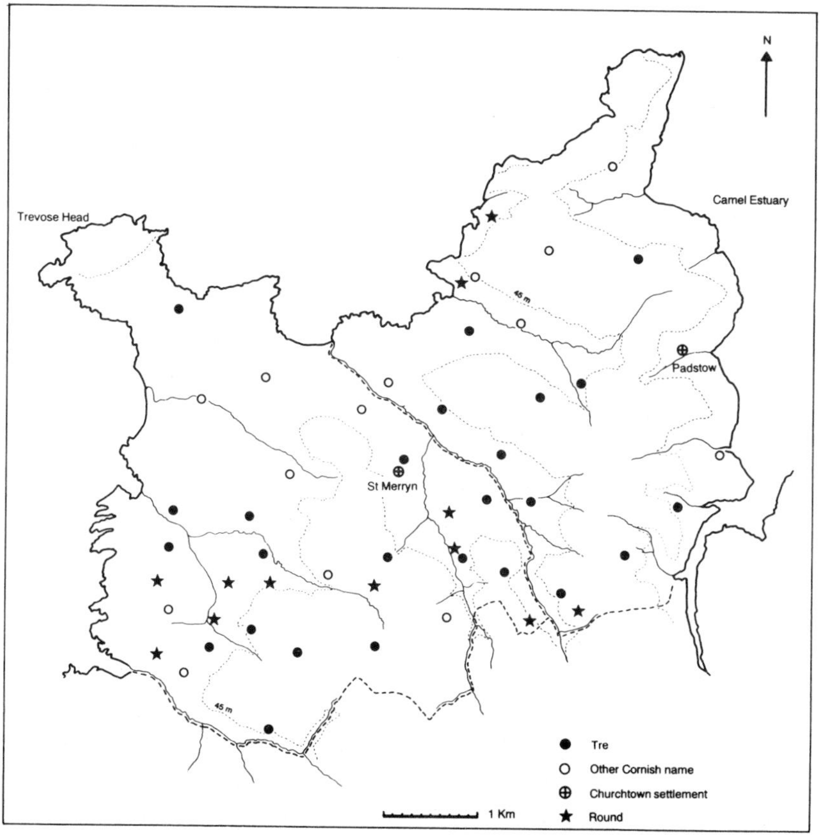

Fig. 3.4 Padstow and St Merryn parishes; late prehistoric enclosures and medieval settlements. (Centred SW 88 74)

so. If that is the case then the degree of change in the countryside between the fourth and seventh centuries must have been even more profound than suggested in the model above. However, there are various points we should note. First, we know from the excavated rounds that the fourth to sixth centuries do act as a cut-off point, in that rounds have yet to be shown to be deserted later than that date; but they were also established and abandoned at various dates over the Iron Age and Romano-British period (Quinnell 1986, p. 124). Second, examples of enclosures set close together are not rare (Johnson and Rose 1982, p. 199, Fig. 4); it may be this relationship that is sometimes perpetuated when a round is close to an early medieval settlement, where one settlement has been abandoned and the other has continued. Furthermore some enclosures may have had a particular status or function which made their siting and subsequent history distinct from those of the other settlements (for example, Golden and Carvossa in Fig. 3.3; Carlyon 1987). These factors will blur the relationship between late Roman and early medieval (and will hinder attempts at statistical analysis).

Before turning to examples in West Penwith another point should be made. The deserted enclosures indicate a change both in settlement pattern and in settlement type: at some point, presumably from the fourth to sixth centuries but conceivably later, the ideas of social organization encapsulated in the defensible enclosure had become redundant. These changing concepts may be to do with the way in which the enclosure reflected the social unity of the occupants (e.g. a kin group); or the need for defence in a society which lacked central control for law enforcement and the peaceful settling of disputes; or the use of defences to express the status of the occupants. Social and political change which affected any of these precepts could be behind the demise of the round.

In addition to the need for a greater understanding of the social and economic context of rounds, various lines of enquiry are brought out by the model. Environmental evidence may indicate whether there were significant changes in land use at the end of the Roman period, for example regeneration of woodland and scrub (and it may be relevant to note that some rounds are found in woodland today). We should be looking for more concrete evidence than we have at present for Romano-British settlements beneath farms with early medieval place-names. We should also be seeking dating evidence for the redundancy of defences: in the light of our model it should be borne in mind that whilst the abandoned rounds did not continue in use beyond the fourth to sixth centuries, this need not mean that defences became redundant at this date on those settlements which continued in use (though this may be likely). It also remains to be established whether unenclosed settlements are a major feature of the repertoire of Romano-British settlements throughout Cornwall as they are in West Penwith (see below) or whether there were marked local traditions, reflecting local variation in social organization and settlement type.

West Penwith provides a different perspective because of the special quality of the archaeological landscape and the nature of its survival. As well as the rounds there are unenclosed settlements of courtyard houses, Romano-British settlements mostly of the second to fourth centuries (Quinnell 1986). In concept they are very similar to the medieval settlements. First, the houses are found both individually and clustered as hamlets, suggesting a similar degree of communal organization. But at the same time each courtyard house is a self-contained unit, like the farms in a medieval hamlet, with the main house plus a number of ancillary buildings.

Survey of large areas by the Cornwall Archaeological Unit and the National Trust has shown how the settlements sit within strongly lynchetted rectilinear field systems which extend for hundreds of hectares and have been perpetuated through the centuries to form the basis of today's working countryside. In outline the Romano-British and medieval patterns are little different both in the character of the settlements and the nature of the land use, a countryside filled with a pattern of hamlets and single farms set in extensive irregular rectilinear field systems, but also with access to large areas of rough grazing on the upland spine.

In looking at the relationship between courtyard houses and medieval settlements the model outlined earlier can be usefully applied by thinking of them as components of the same pattern of settlement. In Figure 3.5 the courtyard house settlements of Carn Euny and Goldherring appear to be part of the overall medieval pattern, in which settlements are spaced at intervals of 450–800 m. Carn Euny and Goldherring are the only settlements above 150 m (490 ft) and may be regarded as relatively marginal settlements which have gone out of use (in the fourth century at Carn Euny, and apparently later at Goldherring; Christie 1978; Guthrie 1969), whilst the others have continued to the present day. In other words, a large proportion of the medieval settlements should be on the site of courtyard houses. Indeed courtyard house settlements probably give us a good idea of the general character to be expected of the unenclosed settlements that emerged at the beginning of the early medieval period.

The third courtyard house settlement in Figure 3.5, at Nanjulian, has a similar context and seems to belong to a chain of settlements spaced along the coastal plateau. At Escalls, Trevedra, Tregiffian and Gurland the hypothetical Romano-British settlements continued in use but the next settlement, 400 m to the north (i.e. Nanjulian), was deserted. Subsequently the present settlement of Nanjulian was established in the valley bottom to the north, though the field system was maintained.

The distance of courtyard house settlements from the nearest medieval settlement ranges from 50 to 750 m, with 400 m as a median. (This compares with 550 m as the median for the distance between a small sample of medieval settlements in the area of Figure 3.5, and may suggest that the courtyard house settlements belong to a denser pattern of settlement). Most courtyard settlements (fifteen of the twenty-five firmly identified sites) are 400 m or more from the nearest medieval settlement and appear to be part of that medieval pattern. Of the remainder, one, Trewern (SW 428 322), is so close to the medieval settlement as to suggest settlement shrinkage, whilst the others may reflect a shift in settlement location, perhaps resulting from desertion followed by re-occupation, as may be the case at Nanjulian. Where early medieval and Romano-British settlements are close together this may sometimes reflect the density of the Romano-British pattern, with

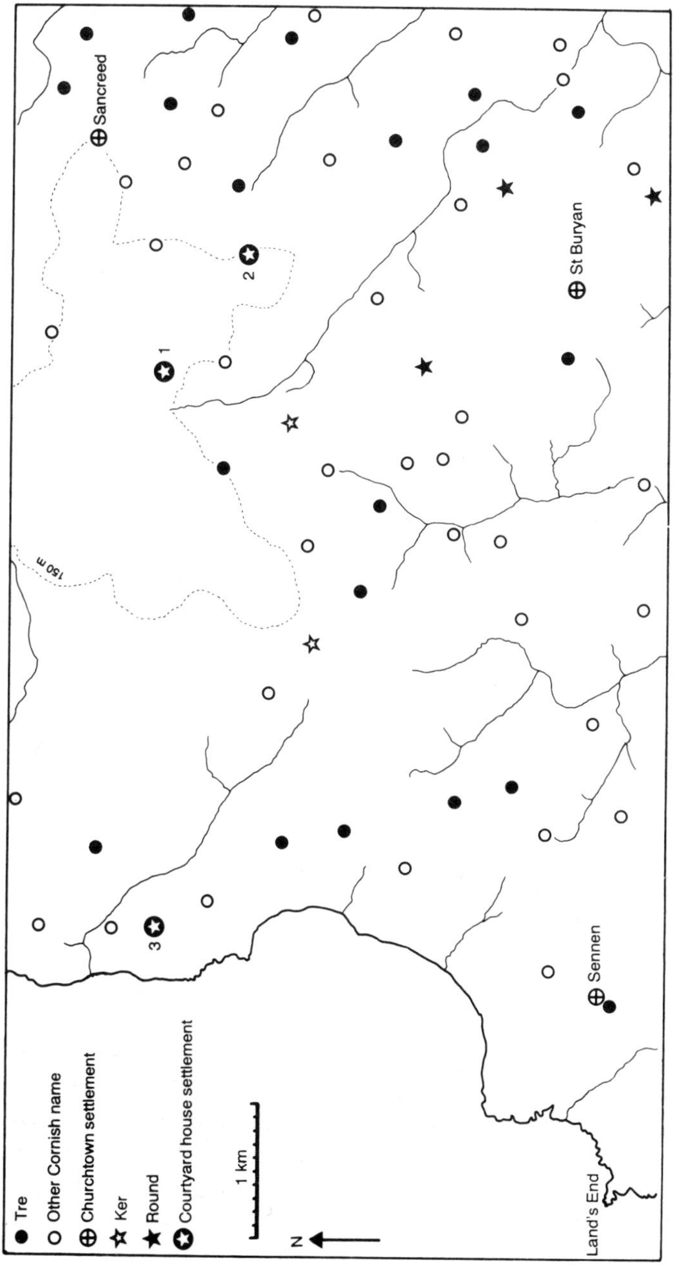

Fig. 3.5 Settlement patterns at Land's End: late prehistoric enclosures, courtyard house settlements and documented medieval settlements. 1: Carn Euny; 2: Goldherring; 3: Nanjulian. (Centred SW 385 275)

courtyard house settlements clustered in the same way that medieval settlements can be paired, e.g. Higher and Lower Bosistow, Boscarn and Boscarn Vean.

It is worth emphasizing that, seen in the context of a general continuum of settlement, the existence of a considerable number of deserted courtyard house settlements is a phenomenon signifying a marked phase of dislocation in the countryside; by comparison, for example, deserted *medieval* settlements are extremely rare in West Penwith.

In summary, we can see evidence for a dense settlement pattern developing during the Romano-British period, both in West Penwith and elsewhere in Cornwall. During say the fifth and sixth centuries (according to our model) there is a retraction in that pattern, with many settlements deserted but most continuing or shifting only slightly, to become the *trefs* etc. of the early medieval period. Subsequently (i.e. between the sixth and fourteenth centuries) many of the abandoned areas and holdings were reoccupied, but perhaps with the new settlement in a slightly different location.

The context for this may be seen in the political, social and economic changes that came about with the end of a relatively stable and to some degree centralized Roman rule. If, coupled to that stability, the tin industry had boosted local prosperity and population during the Roman period (Quinnell 1986, p. 130) then the opposite may now have been true. The fifth century was potentially a period of political instability, uncertainty and change, leading by the sixth century to the development of a Christian British kingdom, a proto-state, with links with the Eastern Roman Empire; perhaps it was the emergence of a more centralized system of government at this time, coupled with changes in social hierarchy and land tenure, that led to the redundancy of rounds as a settlement type. The political fluidity of the period is also suggested by cross-sea contacts and movements of people, attested by the presence of the Welsh Irish, as indicated by their names and Ogham inscriptions on early Christian memorials, and also by the migrations to Brittany, probably by the beginning of the sixth century (Todd 1987, pp. 238–40). What was the scale of this movement, and did it have any effect on the pattern of land use in Cornwall?

Even Cornwall, though apparently little touched by Romanization, was part of the economic and social system of the Roman Empire and was not immune from the effects of the collapse of that system at the beginning of the fifth century (Esmonde Cleary 1989). This was a dynamic period with political and religious change and even migrations. All this may have had a more dramatic effect on the countryside than one might have supposed, but in spite of this, what emerged during the early medieval period must be seen as essentially a continuation and development of that Romano-British pattern.

Acknowledgements

This essay is based on data contained in the Cornwall Archaeological Unit Sites and Monuments Record, in particular information on place-names derived from Oliver Padel's Place-Name Index, compiled for the Institute of Cornish Studies. Helpful comments on our first draft were provided by Nicholas Johnson, Oliver Padel and Henrietta Quinnell.

References

Austin, D., Gerrard, G.A.M. and Greeves, T.A.P., 1989. 'Tin and agriculture in the middle ages and beyond: landscape archaeology in St Neot Parish, Cornwall', *Cornish Archaeology*, 28, pp. 4–251.

Bruce-Mitford, R.L.S., 1956. 'A Dark Age settlement at Mawgan Porth, Cornwall', in *Recent Archaeological Excavations in Britain*, ed. R.L.S. Bruce-Mitford (London).

Carlyon, P.M., 1987. 'Finds from the earthwork at Carvossa, Probus', *Cornish Archaeology*, 26, pp. 103–41.

Christie, P.M., 1978. 'The excavation of an Iron Age souterrain and settlement at Carn Euny, Sancreed, Cornwall', *Proceedings of the Prehistoric Society*, 44, pp. 309–434.

Darby, H.C., 1967. 'The south-western counties', in *The Domesday Geography of South-West England*, ed. H.C. Darby and R. Welldon Finn (Cambridge).

Edwards, N., 1990. *The Archaeology of Early Medieval Ireland* (London).

Esmonde Cleary, A.S., 1989. *The Ending of Roman Britain* (London).

Guthrie, A., 1969. 'Excavation of a settlement at Goldherring, Sancreed, 1958–1961', *Cornish Archaeology*, 8, pp. 5–39.

Herring, P.C., 1986. 'An exercise in landscape history: Pre-Norman and medieval Brown Willy and Bodmin Moor, Cornwall', unpublished MPhil thesis, Sheffield University.

Johnson, N. and Rose, P., 1982. 'Defended settlement in Cornwall: an illustrated discussion', in *The Romano-British Countryside, Studies in Rural Settlement and Economy*, ed. D. Miles, Br Archaeol Rep, Br ser, 103 (i), pp. 151–208.

Johnson, N. and Rose, P., 1994. *Bodmin Moor, an Archaeological Survey. Vol. 1: The human landscape to c. 1800*. RCHME (London).

Leech, R., 1982. 'The Roman interlude in the south-west. The dynamics of economics and social change in Romano-British south Somerset and north Dorset', in *The Romano-British Countryside, Studies in Rural Settlement and Economy*, ed. D. Miles, Br Archaeol Rep, Br ser, 103 (i) pp. 209–67.

Miles, H. and T., 1973. 'Excavations at Trethurgy, St Austell: interim report', *Cornish Archaeology*, 12, pp. 25–30.

Nature Conservancy Council, 1986. *Cornwall Inventory of Ancient Woodland* (Peterborough).

Padel, O.J., 1985. *Cornish Place-Name Elements*, English Place-Name Society, 56–57 (Nottingham).

Pounds, N.J.G., 1947. 'The historical geography of Cornwall', unpublished PhD thesis, University of London.

Preston-Jones, A. and Rose, P., 1986. 'Medieval Cornwall', *Cornish Archaeology*, 25, pp. 135–85.

Quinnell, H., 1986. 'Cornwall during the Iron Age and the Roman period', *Cornish Archaeology*, 25, pp. 111–34.

Rackham, O., 1986. *The History of the Countryside* (London).

Ravenhill, W.L.D., 1967. 'Cornwall' in *The Domesday Geography of South-West England*, ed. H.C. Darby and R. Welldon Finn (Cambridge).

Todd, M., 1987. *The South West to AD 1000* (London).

CHAPTER FOUR

Aspects of Rural Settlement in Northern Britain

Colleen E. Batey

Introduction

Before attempting to discuss this broad-ranging topic, it is necessary to define some of the parameters involved. The geographical area examined will encompass northern England (more specifically the sites of Simy Folds in Teesdale, Ribblehead in Craven and Bryant's Gill in Cumbria), the limited evidence from the Isle of Man and several sites in northern and western Scotland—on both the mainland and the islands. The link between these areas is their potential Norse affinities in settlement forms, which are clearly defined in Scotland, but less clearly so in northern England. It is hoped that by examining individual elements of the settlement units in each area, it might be possible to assess the degree of Scandinavian influence, and to see whether in fact we should only be using with care the term 'Viking Age' to define them. This chapter combines the information in papers given at two conferences: one in Dublin, 'Domestic Architecture in Europe 500–1100', held in 1988, and one held in Exeter in December 1990.

The area encompassed in this essay is generally lacking in prolific tree growth: in the period of Scandinavian influence northern Scotland was apparently as treeless as today, as was presumably the case at Ribblehead (*c.*340 m OD) and at Simy Folds (351 m OD), although no doubt scrubby vegetation and stunted trees (alder in particular) were present. Indeed, the decline in tree pollen and the lack of regeneration has been interpreted as an anthropogenic intervention at Simy Folds; it is possible that the trees were felled for building purposes (Donaldson 1983, p. 17). The lack of available timber which might have been suited to building is of crucial significance to our understanding of the form and perhaps size of the building remains. Although clearly both turf and timber were used in the construction of the buildings, the plentiful supply of building stone—limestone blocks, whinstone or Caithness flagstone for example—ensure the survival of spectacular although ruinous remains, seldom seen in areas where good building timber was readily available.

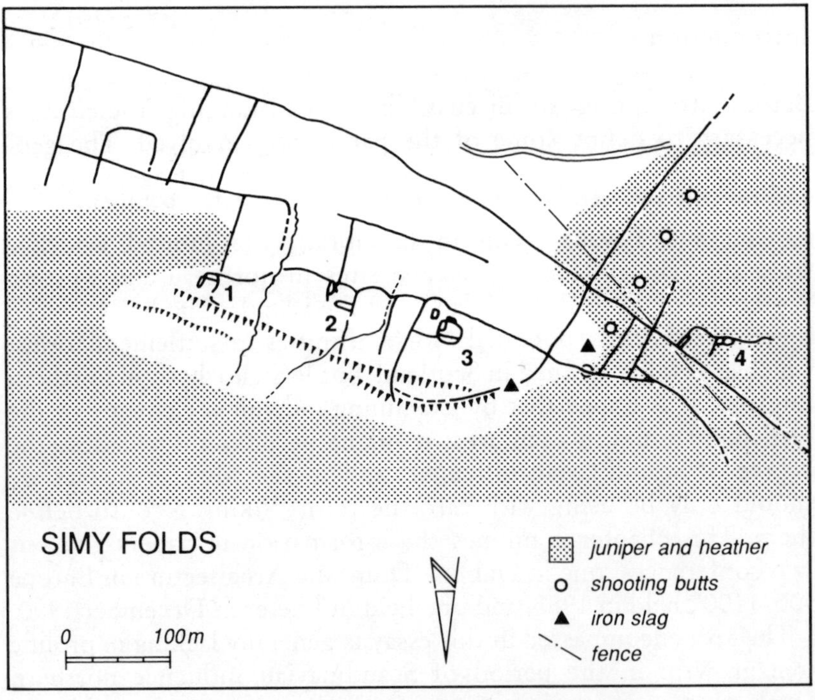

Fig. 4.1 Simy Folds. General plan of settlement. (From Coggins, Fairless and Batey 1983)

The Situation in Northern England

Excavations were undertaken at Simy Folds in Upper Teesdale between 1976 and 1981. A series of small settlement units comprising two to three structures had been identified by Denis Coggins on a north-facing terrace, Holwick Fell, at 351 m OD (Fig. 4.1). Through excavation, two of the four groups identified were examined in some detail and a third had more limited investigation. A potential fifth site, lying some distance to the east, has since been identified and virtually destroyed by work on the access track. Prior to excavation, it was clear that the groups of structures were associated with a series of field boundaries, and in some areas it was clear that these all overlay earlier land divisions along the length of the terrace. Excavation revealed that, at each of the sites examined, a single long narrow building with paved floor was accompanied by one smaller building in the case of the most westerly example, Site 1 (Fig. 4.2), and two small structures at Site 2, to its east, each associated with a paved courtyard area. Differing functions for each of the structures were suggested—dwellings, kitchen and probable stores being identified—although generally lacking diagnostic artefactual material. The western settlement group was characterized by the recovery of a large amount of smithing slag and it was natural to suggest some such activity taking place there during the occupation phase. This was clearly not the case at the other sites examined (Coggins et al. 1983). The uncalibrated C14 determinations from the site suggest a dating of *c*.740–780 ad (see below).

The site of Ribblehead was identified and excavated by Alan King between 1975 and 1976. Located amongst scenery abounding in clints and grykes, he identified a cluster of three structures: a long narrow dwelling, a building identified as a kitchen and a 'workshop', all around a paved courtyard (Fig. 4.3). As with Simy Folds, a pattern of associated field divisions was identified, in this case covering in excess of 1.21 hectares (3 acres) and bounded in part by an enclosure bank. A small series of rather more diagnostic artefacts were recovered at the site, including four coins (one of Wylfhere, Archbishop of York AD 867) which provide a *terminus*

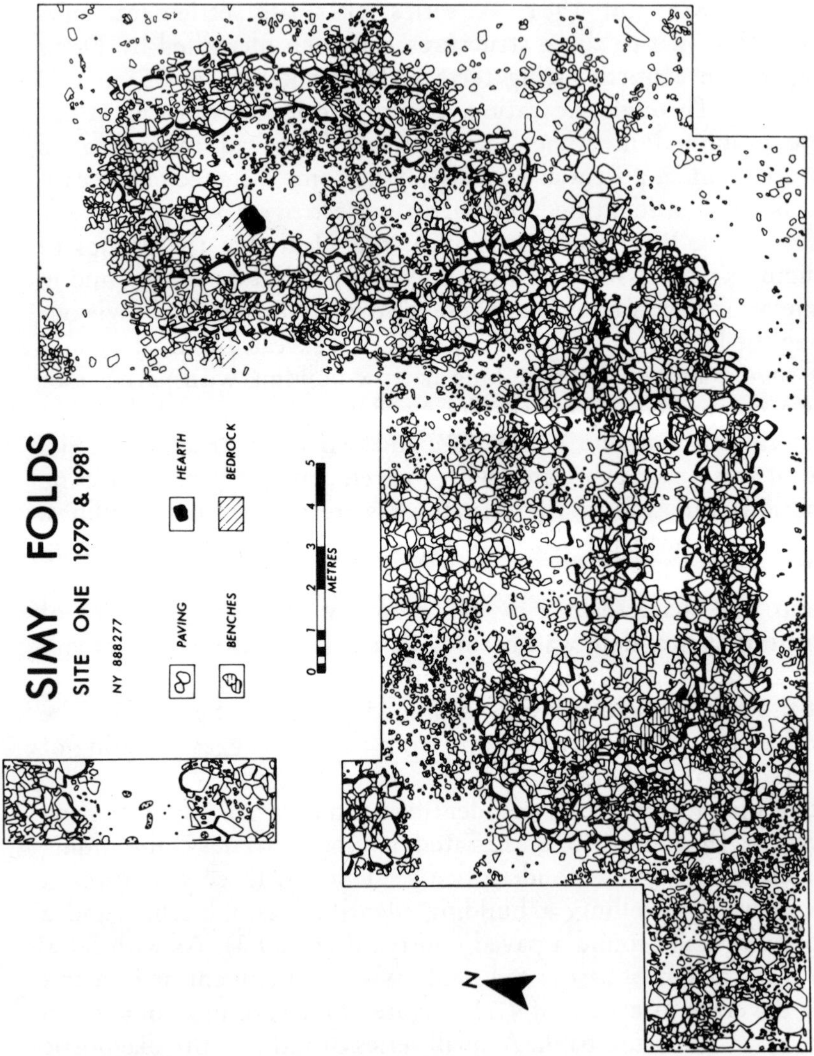

Fig. 4.2 Simy Folds. Plan of Site 1. (From Coggins, Fairless and Batey 1983)

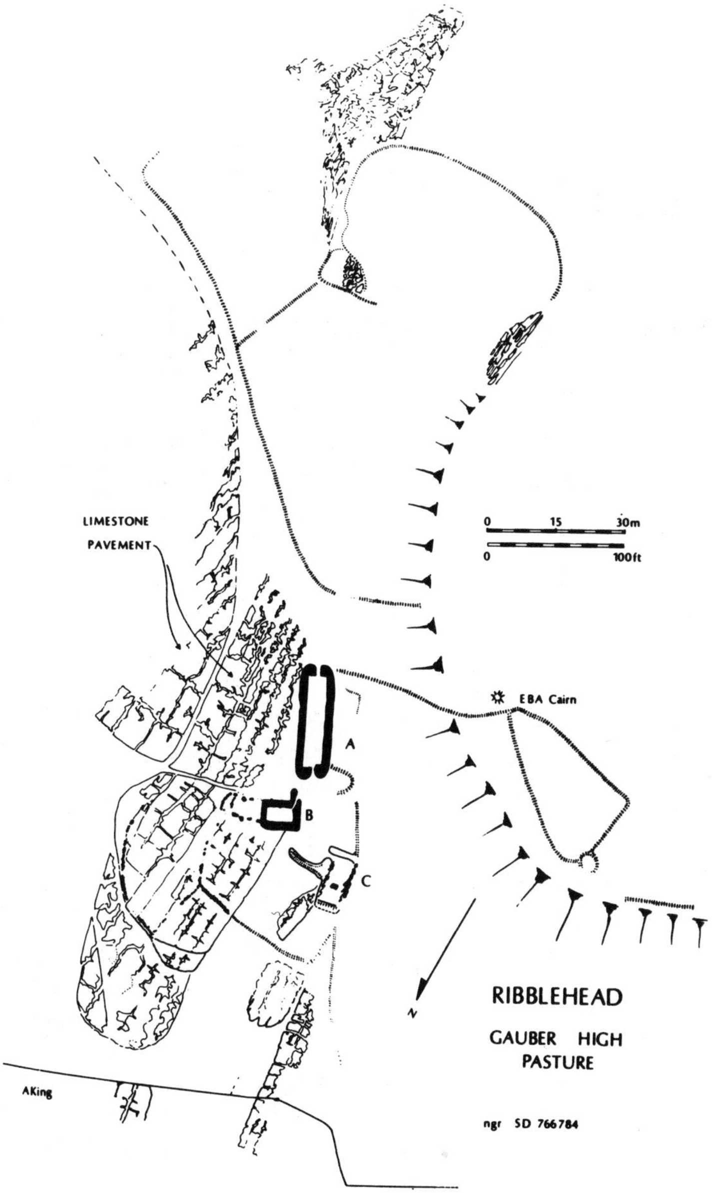

Fig. 4.3 Plan of Ribblehead. (From King 1978)

post quem for the site (King 1978, p. 25). It is, however, worth pointing out that the context for the coins may in fact have been disturbed by earlier trenching on the site by Raistrick, and may not be as reliable as hoped initially. I am particularly grateful for the information supplied by RCHME concerning unpublished comments and for a recent survey at the site, which indicates extensive, although undated, field systems and structures in the vicinity (report SD77NE12 with SD77NE2, SE77NE14, SD77NE15). King has also noted a site at Braida Garth in Kingsdale with a similar complex of sub-rectangular structures and traces of enclosures (King 1970, illus 84–5, 90).

The site of Bryant's Gill in Kentmere, at 290 m OD, was examined by Steve Dickinson between 1981 and 1984. Set amidst a field system covering some 20 hectares, a long narrow structure with associated paved areas, wall footings and postholes was examined. A series of artefacts of rather greater variety than identified at either of the two preceding sites and charcoal providing a provisional C14 determination of 700 ± 80 ad (uncalibrated) might suggest a similar date range to that for Simy Folds, if not Ribblehead (Dickinson 1985).

So, can these various settlement traces be described as Scandinavian? Can they be considered as homes for Scandinavians or simply the homes of the non-Vikings living next door? The uncalibrated dates here quoted would perhaps suggest that they might simply be part of an upland phenomenon owing little to Scandinavian influence, but it is clear that there are certainly similarities in building form, plan and construction between the two areas examined.

Settlement Layout

In order to compare the evidence from Simy Folds and Ribblehead (and to a lesser extent that from Bryant's Gill) with that available from the demonstrably Scandinavian buildings and settlements, it is necessary to examine the individual elements of the settlements remaining. Simy Folds, for example, is a series of settlement units, potentially although not conclusively contemporary, and each serving a different function. Ribblehead appears to be an isolated farmstead, with buildings of differing functions, although it is clear from recent fieldwork by RCHME that there are more remains in the immediate vicinity than previously recorded, although of probable earlier date.

Elsewhere in the 'Viking' areas of north Britain, the range of buildings identified is extensive, including dwelling houses, byres (sometimes integral in the buildings termed 'longhouses'), barns/storehouses, smithies, baths, and in some cases, although not the subject of this paper, small chapels.

In Scotland, the settlement clusters of Freswick, Birsay, Jarlshof and the Udal, for example, are interesting but perhaps misleading. These are areas which have had extensive area excavation. Other sites, such as Sandwick (Bigelow 1978, 1979, 1985), Underhoull (Small 1966) and Drimore Machair (Maclaren 1974) have had more restricted attention, but indications are that these too were not the isolated type of farmstead noted by Small in the North Atlantic context. At Underhoull, Small records the discovery of Norse artefacts and midden further around the bay, indicating settlement which was not further examined (Small 1966, p. 247). At Sandwick, Bigelow notes the recovery of artefacts at three distinct locations around the bay (Bigelow 1978, p. 1). At Drimore Machair, the published plan may indicate further structural remains attached to those excavated but missed by the restricted excavation area (Maclaren 1974, Fig. 1, p. 10). The limited Viking structural evidence from the site at Buckquoy (Ritchie 1977, pp. 184–89) also produced evidence for three dwellings rather than an individual one. These are thought by the excavator to be of different phases, and Ritchie suggests that there were probably other structure(s) in association.

Small has noted that 'the growth of clustered settlement appears to be peculiarly Scottish in the Viking context, the single dispersed farmstead being characteristic of the Faroes, Iceland and Greenland' (Small 1971, p. 79). This would appear to be the natural response to the occupation of an area which could support a relatively large number of people, although it must be remembered that it is very difficult to establish how many of the structures at each site were occupied at the same time—even at such a small site as Simy Folds—and just how many people are represented at each settlement concentration. In upland areas, it is also of crucial importance to bear in mind that settlement units may not be occupied throughout the year, but that some seasonal activity may well have a bearing on the form and/or function of the buildings.

It cannot be judged from all sites whether they were associated with yards, paved areas or field boundaries as at Simy Folds, Ribblehead, Sandwick or Jarlshof (Hamilton 1956, Fig. 79, pp. 170–71). Often the area around the actual building may not be available for excavation as at Buckquoy, Birsay or Drimore. At Freswick, Caithness, the recovery of areas with cultivation marks at the seaward edge of the site, although not all of Norse derivation (Morris et al. 1995), could suggest differential use of areas of the site, and as such there could be evidence of boundaries between. It is, however, not common in the Scottish material to see settlements laid out as if of a single build, although Sigrid Kaland notes similarities in Norway (pers. comm.).

The overall plan of the buildings recovered by Curle and Childe at Freswick (Curle 1939; Childe 1943) indicates a linear extension of rectangular buildings constructed gable on to the coast, a form common in northern regions. Within the complex of buildings excavated by Curle, there is a single exception to the east–west orientation, with Building VII lying at right angles to the rest of the complex. Such a change in alignment has been noted at two other sites in the north: Jarlshof, Shetland (Hamilton 1956, Figs 51 and 61) between Phases I and II, and the Brough of Birsay, Orkney (e.g. Hunter and Morris 1981, Fig. 2; Hunter 1986, ill. 60), where most buildings lie down the slope with a few examples at right angles to them. At this latter site, Hunter would suggest climatic reasons behind the reorientation of the buildings (Hunter 1986, p. 147), and has suggested a total rebuilding programme rather than piecemeal redevelopment (Hunter 1983). This is difficult to prove at the other sites, but Small (1966, p. 237) has drawn attention to the need for the gable of the building to be in the face of the prevailing wind for insulation. This is very clearly demonstrated at Simy Folds in Teesdale.

The complexities of rebuilding on the same site with some of the same stone are indicated at many of the Scottish sites, if not so clearly on the north English sites: it is a common feature which often robs us of a clear understanding of structural sequences.

Construction Methods and Materials

The most obvious remains of the buildings recovered are of stone and generally of rectangular or sub-rectangular form. However, the actual construction methods of the walls at some of the dwellings examined do vary, including use of both beach pebbles and coursed stonework. The form and building method in Scotland is very distinct in comparison to the indigenous Pictish forms in Scotland! The walls are commonly built with interior and exterior facings, a core of mixed soil and rubble (sometimes with turf and stone exterior) and are 1–1.5 m thick. The use of beach stones was recorded at Freswick in Building VI (Curle 1939, Plates XLIII, 1 and 2), where the north, east and west walls are of water-worn beach pebbles in a double line. The south wall, which is later, is of coursed slabs for the most part, over the beach pebbles and sometimes incorporating them in the construction. The eastern end, however, has a variation in that it is a complete mixture of pebbles with coursed stone. This has also been noted at Drimore Machair (Maclaren 1974, Plate 1) and at Jarlshof (Hamilton 1956, Plate XIXc).

The use of slabs in the construction of the walls can easily be seen in many of the northern sites—Freswick, Jarlshof, Sandwick and Beachview, Birsay. It is possible that the basal courses of beach pebbles were superimposed by slabs, in the manner described by Ritchie (1977, p. 197) and as seen today in Caithness. There are problems in the consideration of the structures at several sites because of extensive robbing of the walls, as at Bryant's Gill. However, it is clear at Simy Folds and Ribblehead that the suitability and plentiful nature of the local stone has led to the preservation of a reasonable height of the structures (between 0.5 and 1 m), despite collapse. The wall construction at Simy Folds does show traces of both rubble construction, i.e. having very little actual structure, and also the use of inner and outer 'skins' with rubble infill. This is apparent, in particular, in the western wall of the long building at Site 1, where the wall had been deliberately thickened by adding to the inner face of the 'sandwich' form wall (Coggins et al. 1983, p. 12). Ribblehead's walling has been described as 'rubble-built'. The stability of the structure is of significance when assessing a possible superstructure for the building. The apparent relative instability of these walls could be caused by the weathering out from them of any turf bonding elements.

The use of clay bedding for walling, as seen in the southern wall of Building VI at Freswick (Curle notebook NMRS MS 28a (SAS 461), p. 14) and in Childe's wall PQ (1943, p. 7) is interesting and can be paralleled at the Brough of Birsay (Hunter 1983; Hunter and Morris 1981, p. 250), in addition to the use of foundation trenches noted there. A variation of this can be seen at Simy Folds, where instead of a clay bedding, a clay bank has been retained for the wall to be built upon, and the inner part of the house appears to be correspondingly sunken. There is a similar situation at Ribblehead, where the undulating bedrock has been used to the same effect in Building C (King 1978, p. 21).

At present, it seems to be the case that the earlier Viking structures in the north of Scotland had walls essentially made of rounded beach pebbles with rubble infill between the two parallel rows and possibly in some cases—as for example at the Brough of Birsay (Cruden 1965, pp. 26–7)—evidence for alternating turf and stone exterior wall faces. Hunter notes that the earlier Viking buildings in his area of excavation on the Brough of Birsay are very well built, of good quality masonry and land preparation, in addition to having good drainage precautions of deep channels. The need for structural stability meant differing construction methods were required for the long and short walls, and a stepping of the inner part of the wall. In the eleventh century he notes a decline in standards, with the 'structural modifications having been persistently botched' (Hunter 1986, p. 143) and only surviving today where they had been superimposed on earlier walling at foundation level.

Although some buildings seem to exhibit a bow-shaped form, such as Udal, and the Brough of Birsay (e.g. Cruden 1965, p. 26, Fig. 2 period 1), several others do not, and indeed walling collapse has in several cases given a misleading impression. This is clearly the case at the Braaid in the Isle of Man, a site termed 'a typical Norse farmstead' (Cubbon 1983, p. 18), where two roughly rectangular structures were excavated: these are juxtaposed with a large circular stone structure which is likely to be pre-Norse in date.

Since several structures at other sites seem to have had an internal width of between 3 and 6 m it has been suggested that a single central row of postholes with the roof bedded directly onto the wall top would have been sufficient. Entrances are found in varying locations—opposing in the long walls or singly in one gable, depending on function or the direction of the prevailing wind. Where the evidence survives, it would seem that the northern English sites had entrances at the narrow end away from the prevailing wind, unless there was a suggestion of interconnection between buildings, as with Simy Folds 2, where a path led between the two small structures which had entrances in the side walls.

Most of the structural evidence does, however, come from buildings with coursed stone walls and perhaps in this respect our information is biased. In Scotland the sites examined are Late Norse; Westness, Beachview Birsay, Freswick and Orphir, for example, are often apparently of high status and as such may be atypical. Here walls are often more upstanding, up to 1 m or more in many cases, and it is consequently easier to talk about the actual form of the building itself. From this category we can learn of variations in byre doors as at Sandwick where there is a characteristic broadening of the exit for the cows; while at Beachview Birsay parallel walling survives probably as a replacement or buttress (Morris 1983).

At Freswick, the buildings seem to lack opposing entrances, unlike examples at Jarlshof (Hamilton 1956, Fig. 79, Building 1) and at Sandwick (Bigelow 1985, p. 110). This may be related to the lack of cattle space within the building. The buildings at Freswick are square cornered, differing from some other northern examples, such as Drimore (Maclaren 1974, Fig. 1), Buckquoy (Ritchie 1977, Fig. 3) and Underhoull (Small 1966, Fig. 10), which may be of earlier date and which has a decidedly rounded form to the gable. The differences may be a response to differing roofing construction, with the curving ends possibly representing a hipped gable, as suggested at Ribblehead (King 1978, p. 25). The distribution of the postholes in Building VI at Freswick could indicate an aisled construction, as at Jarlshof (Hamilton 1956, pp. 107, 160) where the buildings are generally squared at the gable ends. Of the few remaining postholes at Sandwick, the indications are that they supported a central ridge-pole (Bigelow 1978, Fig. 2) and at Underhoull Small notes a similar distribution (1966, Fig. 10), although only two were recovered on the central axis. In addition, an unpublished aisled building from Radford's excavations on the Brough of Birsay has been distinguished (Morris, pers. comm.).

A major problem for an understanding of the superstructure of these buildings is the likelihood that at least part of the roofing structure was supported by the walling (suggested by Hunter at Birsay Building III, 1986, p. 84) or by posts internally which may have been supported on post-pads, as part of the paved floor. This was suggested as being the case at Simy Folds (Coggins et al. 1983, p. 20). Since some of the excavations noted here were undertaken many years ago, such apparently insignificant single flat slabs may well not have been recorded. This may have been the case at Freswick, for example, where the only available complete excavation plan of Building VI was drawn on the penultimate day of the excavation, resulting in such secondary features as a cross-wall not being recorded (Batey 1987, p. 78); so it is highly likely that isolated flat stones may have gone unnoticed, particularly where the recorded floor level does in fact pre-date the standing walls!

The use of flat slabs to form level, or levelling, surfaces is also worthy of note. At the eastern end of Building IV at Freswick the pathway was levelled up by flat slabs, very much as it was at Underhoull (Small 1966, p. 239). The floor of the smithy was also carefully made up of flat slabs (Curle 1939, p. 81), but elsewhere flagging was used to cover drains. Extensive use of flat slabs was employed at Simy Folds and Ribblehead, not only as flagging in the main buildings but also in entrance ways and, in the case of Simy Folds, as a potential area for grinding corn in the kitchen (Coggins et al. 1983, p. 14).

The use of timber in the construction of the buildings is difficult to quantify. It was suggested that turf and probably timber would have been used at both Ribblehead (King 1978, p. 25) (see Fig. 4.4) and Simy Folds (Coggins et al. 1983, pp. 20–21); in Scotland, at Freswick too, this is poorly documented, apart from the postholes in Building VI which indicate an aisled roofing construction. But what other interior features were of timber? The bed in Building IV was presumably composed of wood, and in Childe's Phase I there are suggestions of stone restraints for timber elements. It is also conceivable that Childe's Phase O may represent a series of post-pads, or part of a turf-clad wall (Batey 1987, p. 83, and Fig. 21B). In the complex examined by Curle, the area between Buildings I and III, delimited by a series of small stones, could represent the base of a timber partition. Recent work in the Faroes by Thorsteinsson (1976) can assist the interpretation of such elements, where evidence of timber panelling, for example, has been noted in excavation. The use of timber in the construction of houses is well documented in Scandinavia, for example at Ullandhaug (Myhre 1980) and in boat houses, such as Stend (Myhre 1976) in Norway. In Faroe as well, work at Kvívík by Dahl (1965, pp. 137–39) provides corroboration of this.

The lack of suitable timber for construction purposes could be overcome in a number of ways. Driftwood as a source of timber is recorded, for example, in excavation at Underhoull (Small 1966, p. 238), at Jarlshof (Hamilton 1956, p. 199), and also at Birsay (Donaldson et al. 1981, p. 80; Hunter 1986, p. 220). At some sites, such as Papa Stour in Shetland, there is evidence for the direct importation of timber for constructional purposes, in that case for a fine timber floor and wall panelling (Crawford 1987, p. 144, Fig. 47), in a building interpreted as a 'stofa'. It was suggested that a raised timber floor may have been in place in one of the buildings

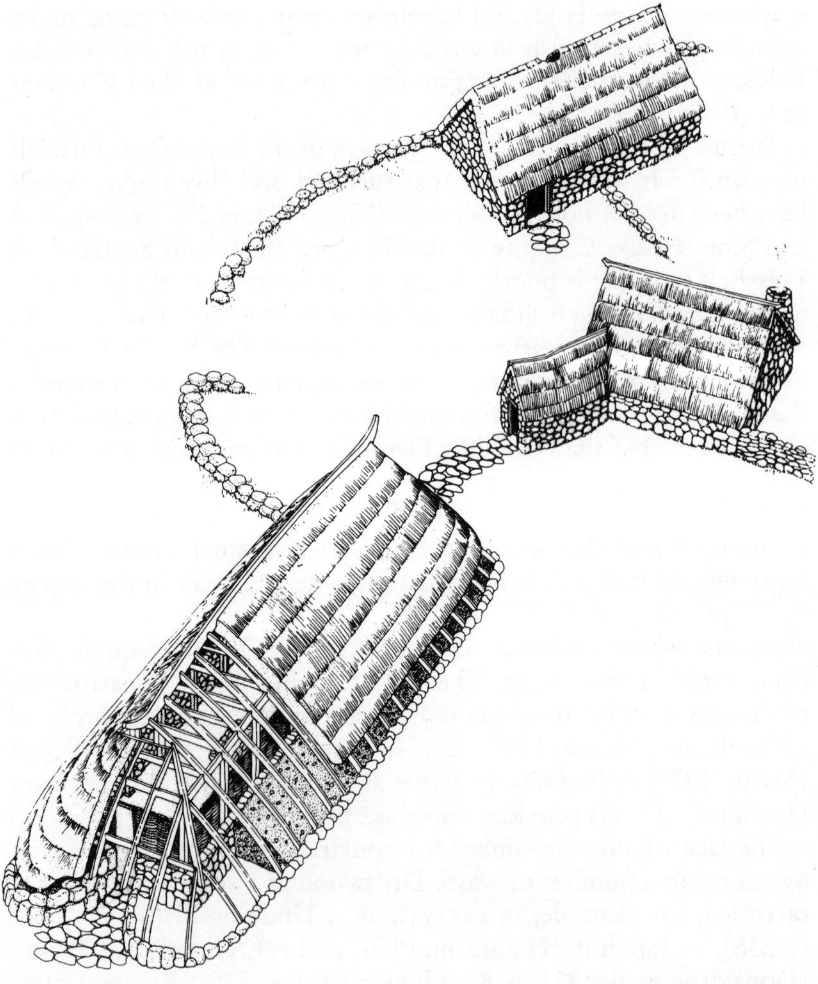

Fig. 4.4 Suggested reconstruction of Ribblehead. (From King 1978)

at Simy Folds (Coggins et al. 1983, p. 14), but a driftwood source can be ruled out here. At the Braaid in the Isle of Man, the large 'boat-shaped' building lacks defined end walls and it has been suggested that these walls were originally of timber (Gelling 1964).

Apart from the potential presence of timber on these northern sites, at Freswick it should be noted that in the western wall of Building VII in Curle's complex the skull of a small whale was located. The use of whalebone for constructional purposes can also be paralleled at Drimore (Maclaren 1974) and Buckquoy (Ritchie 1977, p. 179) in a late Pictish context. Other items employed in the construction of walling or interior features on these sites include the use of a broken quernstone in the kerb of Childe's hearth (1943, p. 7), a feature matched at Simy Folds (Coggins et al. 1983, p. 14).

It is not at present possible to quantify the extent to which turf was used in the buildings of the Norse in Scotland. The resource was there but perhaps the quality of the stone negated its full use, although Small would suggest that much of the Underhoull rebuilding was the result of external wall faces collapsing due to rotting turf, as Cruden suggests in earlier excavations at Birsay.

Building Types and Functions

The range of building uses represented is varied: dwellings, smithy, barn/storehouse, or workshop at Freswick and Jarlshof and at the Brough of Birsay for example; additionally, at the Udal, Crawford records a corn-drying kiln (as at Beachview Birsay) and a threshing floor, metal-working furnaces and the inevitable 'other small buildings of unknown function' (Crawford and Switzur 1977, p. 131). Not all aspects of these functions are represented in the northern English sites, so these features cannot be compared. However, it is salutary to note that a spatial analysis through detailed artefactual analysis by Bigelow at Sandwick in Shetland indicates a zoning of the building, suggesting cattle at one end of the structure and a dwelling at the other. These features may not necessarily always be distinguishable structurally (Bigelow 1985, p. 111).

Dwelling houses without byres

The northern English examples seem to fall within this category of structure. It is not clear whether this was the result of differing economic exploitation of the land, or a simple corollary of a milder climate which did not necessitate overwintering of cattle indoors; although it should be noted that at the Braaid in the Isle of Man, a second rectangular structure at the site was suggested as a possible animal house (Gelling 1964). This assumes that the northern English sites were indeed permanent all year round settlements, which is far from certain. Recent survey work in the Isle of Man by Gillian Quine has shed new light on the extent of the shieling tradition on the island (Quine 1990), and the results surely cannot be ignored in relation to other upland areas.

In Scotland, however, there are several examples where the byre-less type of structure has been identified, both from an early Viking context at Jarlshof in Phase I, the 'Parent Dwelling' (Hamilton 1956, pp. 107ff.), where a separate animal house is noted, as in Structure 17 on the Brough of Birsay (Hunter 1986, pp. 95ff.) and in a Late Norse context at Freswick Links (Building VI) (Batey 1987, pp. 73ff.), where a drain to one end of the house has an unclear function. These structures are of very variable dimensions, such as Jarlshof's 21.3 × 6.1 m, Brough of Birsay's 14 × 6 m and Freswick Links' *c.*12 × 4 m, and they are also of varying layout. Jarlshof, for example, has two opposing entrances and one in the gable, while Freswick Links seems to have had, possibly, one on the southern side and conceivably one in the eastern wall.

Traces of benches have been noted at Jarlshof, possibly at Freswick and certainly in the recent work by Hunter on the Brough of Birsay where the bench edges were of stone rather than the wood suggested elsewhere. Benches were also suggested in the main long building at Simy Folds and at Ribblehead. Generally a hearth was located on the central axis, sometimes eccentrically, as seen clearly at Jarlshof in the western part of the structure, at Birsay as a spread of burning and at Freswick Links at the eastern end of Building VI, in an area where the floor deposit was discoloured. In the Isle of Man, these two features, a central hearth and benches, have been taken as indicators of a Norse origin for the structures at Doarlish Cashen and Cass ny Hawin (see, for example, Cubbon 1983, pp. 18–19). The corner hearths noted at Simy Folds and Ribblehead can be paralleled at Papa Stour, although there is clearly a relation to differing building functions here which does not allow too close an analogy.

Kitchen and workshops

Building B at Ribblehead has been identified as a kitchen or working area (King 1978, p. 25), having evidence of a circular oven or kiln in its north-eastern corner. One of the small buildings at Simy Folds (Building 3, Site 2—see Fig. 4.5) was also interpreted as a kitchen because of the carefully laid setting of stones, suggested as a corn-drying platform, an identification supported by the recovery of a quernstone fragment (Coggins et al. 1983, pp. 12–14).

Only one of the structures examined at Freswick is recorded as having an oven, Building VI of Curle's complex. The type of oven is closely paralleled at Jarlshof (Hamilton 1956, p. 109) where it was located in a suggested kitchen area. This might explain the location of the hearth in Building VI at one end of the structure. A possible similar feature, noted as a stone-lined cooking pit, may be cited from the site at L'Anse aux Meadows in Newfoundland (Ingstad 1977, p. 139).

The incorporation of one kiln, and possibly a second one in the north of Building VII, presumably indicates a building designated specifically for work, but unfortunately the northern end of the building was not examined, so little further can be said of this structure. It cannot be judged whether the kiln(s) was used for parching grain, which could have been stored in that building (or possibly near by in Building II) and dried out within the building on the clay floor; this would have been a good heat conductor (Small 1966, pp. 238–39). However, a clay surface could also have been used as a threshing floor (Fenton 1978, p. 364) which might also explain the presence of grain in that building. The threshing floor from Buckquoy, Birsay, had a paved surface (Ritchie 1977,

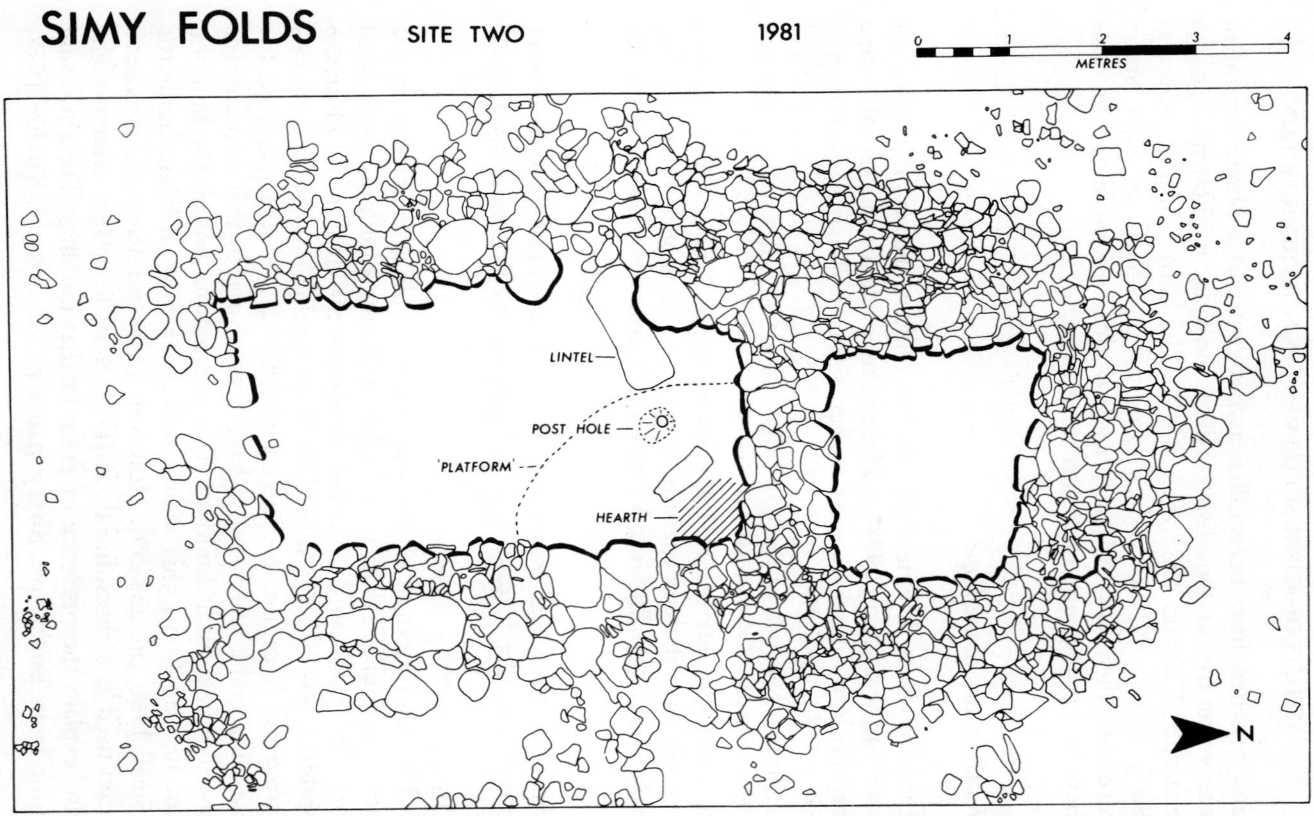

Fig. 4.5 Simy Folds. Building 3, Site 2: the "kitchen". (From Coggins, Fairless and Batey 1983)

p. 186). Alternatively, the kiln could have been used for the drying of fish or the firing of pottery, and Curle did indeed note a large amount of pottery recovered from this building.

Smithy

King identified Building C at Ribblehead as a smithy, an identification supported by the recovery of a central hearth, 'iron-rich cinders and sharpening-cum-hammerstones' (King 1978, p. 25). At Simy Folds the second complex to be examined, lying to the east of the terrace (Site 1), produced only two structures: the large one aligned along the terrace was identified as the working area, with a substantial stone identified as an anvil stone and large amounts of hammerscale being recovered. The small building at right angles to this one had large pieces of slag-like waste on its floor, but more importantly also incorporated into the walls (Coggins et al. 1983, pp. 8–10), suggesting a secondary date to the larger structure.

The pair of conjoining structures at Freswick Links (Building III), identified as a smithy, lay to the west of the complex and, although not fully excavated, produced evidence of extensive industrial activity associated with various phases of a hearth of substantial size (3 × 2.44 m) and flagging. Many other sites in the north have produced similar evidence: for example, at Jarlshof a smithy was located at right-angles to the parent dwelling (Hamilton 1956, pp. 110–11 and Fig. 53). The Jarlshof building was paved and measured 6.4 × 3.05 m and its main feature was a large hearth. There was a further smithy associated with House 4 (Hamilton 1956, pp. 159–60) which replaced an earlier one. It is recorded that this was a production area for bronze pins, the moulds of which were recovered there. Two smithies were therefore noted at Jarlshof, and indeed the same may have been the case at Freswick. One was excavated by Curle (Building III, Curle 1939, pp. 81–82), while another stone building at the northern end of the Links (Shore Ruins, Batey 1987, Plate 9A) is recorded as having slag all over the floor (RCAHMS 1911, no. 49, p. 19).

The presence of a smithy on this and other Viking sites is not unexpected. They are a common feature and have been noted extensively in Iceland, at Skallakot and Stöng, for example (Roussell 1943a, pp. 68–69; b, pp. 84–86), and in Greenland at Garðar (Norlund 1930, pp. 111–12). This element would be expected on a site which would have to be self-sufficient. Evidence for on-site industrial activity has also been recorded at the Brough of Birsay, where Curle has noted extensive activity in the immediately pre-Viking period, with the moulds for copper-alloy pins and brooches being recovered (Curle 1982, pp. 26–39), and Hunter's excavations at the site also indicate iron-working (McDonnell 1986, pp. 198–203). The Udal (Crawford and Switzur 1977, p. 131) and Westness, Rousay (Kaland 1973, p. 84) have produced similar evidence.

A number of narrow vents have been identified at Freswick Links which may have been associated with industrial activity: for example, in Building VI at the western end, in Building IV at the northern and western sides, in Building III leading directly to the hearth and in Building I considerably below the level of the bath house. This disproportionate number of air vents or drains is interesting. Building VI has no definite indications of a byre at the western end, and one in Building III leads to the fire and so cannot be a drain; it is more likely to be a flue. This is similar to an example from Underhoull where it is suggested that it provided a draught for the fire (Small 1966, p. 245). This feature is tentatively identified as being associated with the raising of steam or smoke conceivably in association with the preservation of fish at the site (as indicated by the faunal remains; see, for example, Jones et al. 1983) or industrial activity (Batey 1987, p. 94).

Storehouses

It is possible that the small building (Building 2) on Site 2 at Simy Folds was a storehouse, since it lacked distinctive internal features or a definite hearth (Coggins et al. 1983, p. 6). Storehouses have been tentatively identified at other sites, such as Building II at Freswick. The possible association with Building I may be suggested by the fact that it has apparently only one entrance, that leading from Building I, which was blocked at the time of the building of the bath house. Alternatively, it is possible that the building could have been entered at a higher level than the foundation course, possibly having a raised timber floor, as at Papa Stour, Shetland (Crawford 1987), or Simy Folds (Coggins et al. 1983) perhaps used for storage purposes as described by Borchgrevink (1980) in late medieval Scandinavia. These buildings can vary in size and shape, and buildings which had previously served other functions may subsequently have been used simply as outhouses, there being several examples of this at Jarlshof.

Conclusion

The date range of the structures discussed here is broad. The use of C14 dating at Simy Folds provides determinations of 1210 ± 80 bp to 1170 ± 70 bp giving an uncalibrated dating of 740 ad and 780 ad (Coggins et al. 1983, p. 24). At Ribblehead the dating comes from a small hoard of coins with a *terminus post quem* in the late ninth century. In Scotland, the dating evidence is based on several criteria, ranging from Saga inferences and artefact analysis to C14 (e.g. Crawford and Switzur 1977) and thermoluminescence dating, with the level of dating accuracy increasing with the rapid expansion of recent excavation programmes in the area. Most of the evidence cited here is from sites dated to the Late Norse period (eleventh–thirteenth centuries), although some, such as that from the Brough of Birsay, lies in the true Viking period (late ninth–eleventh centuries).

The form of the building is, however, still an oft-quoted criteria for ascribing a Scandinavian origin to a particular building or building group. The idea that a bow-shaped or sub-rectangular structure has to be Norse in origin is hard to dislodge for the period under consideration. This is despite the fact that in Scandinavia there are buildings of squarer form (as well as more rectangular) in the Viking period, as well as in Dublin and south-west Scotland where the squared form is prevalent. In northern and western Scotland, the distinctive pre-Viking, Pictish structures with a cellular form are replaced by rectangular buildings in a stratigraphical succession, as at the Udal in North Uist and at Buckquoy in Orkney. But what of the roughly rectangular structure at the Wag of Forse in Caithness? This has also been suggested as having a pre-Viking origin (see, for example, Gourlay 1989). The question is not easily answered, and even where excavation has taken place, the results may not be so easy to interpret.

Recently, Richards has noted that 'it is difficult to recognize anything specifically Viking about the Viking Age buildings of England and the Isle of Man. In general the Scandinavian incomers appear to have adopted native building styles . . .' (Richards 1991, p. 69). This statement may well be true but there are strands of evidence which can support a Scandinavian genesis for these structures, as indicated in the course of the paper; the problem is locating clearly dated, culturally diagnostic pre-Viking settlement in this area of England. Manx examples, such as that at Doarlish Cashen, are argued as Norse simply because they are bow-shaped stone and turf buildings with benches and central hearth. Is this a persuasive argument?

In order to argue for a continuum, we need to be able to define what went before. In a masterly summary of the pre-Norse situation in northern England, Higham draws attention to several sites which have produced rectangular or sub-rectangular structures, such as Crosby Ravensworth and earlier phases at Yeavering, and makes the point clearly that there is a possibility of some structures, which may lack distinctive artefactual assemblages, being later shieling sites (Higham 1986, pp. 246ff.).

The evidence outlined here is only part of the material which is currently available. I have touched on questions which may be answerable in the light of ongoing work, but such is the case with any statement based on archaeological evidence. Several of the sites which have initially been considered single structures are likely to be part of larger settlements and, conversely, some of the buildings in the greater complexes of structures are not parts of such large groups, as initially suspected. The range of building functions is important to note because to a certain extent such differences can affect the building form, and, of course, once one loses sight of the functions of the buildings one is really only examining a very incomplete picture.

The stone buildings discussed create one further problem. An examination is being made of *stone* buildings with timber and sometimes turf elements, and this sets the Scottish material in the North Atlantic milieu to which it culturally belongs. It is often very difficult to identify with certainty elements of either timber or turf in these structures, and it is likely therefore that these are under-represented.

The variety of forms and functions of Norse buildings in Scotland is more extensive than superficial examination would suggest. It is clear that, as in Scandinavia and the other Western colonies, one can no longer speak of a typical Viking building. The actual construction of a building may well have as much to do with the availability of local resources as the language spoken or political allegiance of the builders themselves. Sadly, archaeology itself cannot yet always identify the foreigner, especially not if that foreigner is content to continue local traditions. It is only the innovator who can readily be identified in the archaeological record.

References

Baldwin, J.R. and Whyte, I.D., 1985. *The Scandinavians in Cumbria*, Scottish Society for Northern Studies (Edinburgh).

Batey, C.E., 1987. *Freswick Links, Caithness: a Re-appraisal of the Late Norse site in its Context*, Br Archaeol Rep, Br ser, 179, 2 vols (Oxford).

Bekker-Nielsen, H., Foote, P. and Olsen, O. (eds), 1981. *Proceedings of the Eighth Viking Congress* (Århus 1977, Odense).

Bigelow, G.F., 1978. *Preliminary Report of the 1978 Excavations at Sandwick, Unst, Shetland Isles* (Private Distribution).

Bigelow, G.F., 1979. *Excavation of a Norse-Medieval Settlement, Unst, Shetland 1978–79; An Interim Report* (Private Distribution).

Bigelow, G.F., 1985. 'Sandwick, Unst and the Late Norse Shetland economy', in *Shetland Archaeology*, ed. B. Smith (Lerwick), pp. 95–127.

Borchgrevink, A., 1980. 'The houses of the Norwegian "Seters": an analysis of local type variations (pt 1)', *Northern Studies*, 16, pp. 53–69.

Brothwell, D. and Dimbleby, G., (eds), 1981. *Environmental Aspects of Coasts and Islands*, Br Archaeol Rep, Int ser, 94 (Symposia Assoc for Environ Archaeol 1), (Oxford).

Childe, V.G., 1943. 'Another Late Viking house at Freswick, Caithness', *Proc Soc Antiq Scot*, 77, 1942–43, pp. 5–17.

Coggins, D., Fairless, K.J. and Batey, C.E., 1983. 'Simy Folds: an early medieval settlement site in Upper Teesdale, Co Durham', *Medieval Archaeology*, 27, pp. 1–26.

Crawford, B.E., 1987. *Scandinavian Scotland*, Scotland in the Early Medieval Ages, 2 (Leicester).

Crawford, I.A. and Switzur, R., 1977, 'Sandscaping and C14: the Udal, Uist', *Antiquity*, 51, pp. 124–36.

Cruden, S.H., 1965. 'Excavations at Birsay, Orkney', in *Fourth Viking Congress*, ed. A. Small (Edinburgh and London), pp. 22–31.

Cubbon, M., 1983. 'The archaeology of the Vikings in the Isle of Man', in *The Viking Age in the Isle of Man*, ed. C. Fell, et al. (London), pp. 13–26.

Curle, A.O., 1939. 'A Viking settlement at Freswick, Caithness. Report on excavations carried out in 1937 and 1938', *Proc Soc Antiq Scot*, 73, 1938–39, pp. 71–110.

Curle, C.L., 1982. *The Pictish and Norse Finds from the Brough of Birsay 1934–74*, Soc Antiq Scot Monograph 1 (Edinburgh).

Dahl, S., 1965. 'A survey of archaeological Investigations in the Faroes', in *Fourth Viking Congress*, ed. A. Small (Edinburgh and London), pp. 135–41.

Dickinson, S., 1985. 'Bryant's Gill, Kentmere: another 'Viking-period' Ribblehead?', in *The Scandinavian in Cumbria*, ed. J.R. Baldwin and I.D. Whyte (Edinburgh), pp. 83–88.

Donaldson, A. [M]., 1983. 'Pollen analysis', in D. Coggins et al. 'Simy Folds', *Medieval Archaeology*, 27, pp. 16–18.

Donaldson, A.M., Morris, C.D. and Rackham, D.J., 1981. 'The Birsay Bay project preliminary investigations into the past exploitation of the coastal environment of Birsay, Mainland, Orkney', in *Environmental Aspects of Coasts and Islands*, ed. D. Brothwell and G. Dimbleby (Oxford), pp. 65–85.

Fell, C., Foote, P., Graham-Campbell, J. and Thompson, R. (eds), 1983. *The Viking Age in the Isle of Man*, Selected papers from the Ninth Viking Congress, Isle of Man 4–14 July 1981 (London).

Fenton, A., 1978. *The Northern Isles: Orkney and Shetland* (Edinburgh).
Gelling, P.S., 1964. 'Re-excavation of a Viking house at the Braaid', *Journal of the Manx Museum*, 6: 80, pp. 201–5.
Gourlay, R., 1989. 'The Picts', in *The New Caithness Book*, ed. D. Ormand (Wick), pp. 56–66.
Hall, R.A. (ed.), 1982. *Viking Age York and the North*, Counc Br Archaeol, Res Rep 27 (London).
Hamilton, J.R.C., 1956. *Excavations at Jarlshof, Shetland*, MoW Archaeol Rep 1.
Higham, N., 1986. *The Northern Counties to AD 1000; A Regional History of England* (London and New York).
Hunter, J.R., 1983. 'Recent excavations on the Brough of Birsay', *Orkney Heritage*, 2 (Birsay: A Centre of Political and Ecclesiastical Power), pp. 152–170.
Hunter, J.R., 1986. *Rescue Excavations on the Brough of Birsay 1974–82*, Soc Antiq Scot Monograph 4 (Edinburgh).
Hunter, J.R. and Morris, C.D., 1981. 'Recent excavations at the Brough of Birsay, Orkney', in *Proceedings of the Eighth Viking Congress*, ed. H. Bekker-Nielsen et al. (Odense), pp. 245–58.
Ingstad, A.S., 1977. *The Discovery of the Norse Settlement in America. Excavations at L'Anse aux Meadows, Newfoundland, 1961–68*, 1 (Oslo-London-New York).
Jones, A.K.G., Batey, C.E., Morris, C.D. and Rackham, D.J., 1983. 'Man and the environment at Freswick Links: preliminary observations from a Late Norse settlement in Caithness', in *Integrating the Subsistence Economy*, ed. M. Jones, pp. 163–176.
Jones, M.K. (ed.), 1983. *Integrating the Subsistence Economy*, Br Archaeol Rep, Int ser, 181 (Symposia Assoc for Environ Archaeol 4) (Oxford).
Kaland, S.H.H., 1973. 'Westnessutgravninene pa Rousay, orknoyene', *Viking*, 37, pp. 77–101.
King, A., 1970. *Early Pennine Settlement: a Field Study*, Clapham (Yorkshire), via Lancaster.
King, A., 1978. 'Gauber High Pasture, Ribblehead—an interim report', in *Viking Age York and the North*, ed. R.A. Hall (London) pp. 21–25.
Maclaren, A., 1974. 'A Norse house on Drimore Machair, South Uist', *Glasgow Archaeol J*, 3, pp. 9–18.
McDonnell, G., 1986. 'Iron and iron working with technological discussion', in *Rescue Excavations on the Brough of Birsay*, ed. J.R. Hunter (Edinburgh), pp. 198–203.
Meldrum, E. (ed.), 1971. *The Dark Ages in the Highlands* (Inverness).

Morris, C.D., 1983. 'Excavations around the Bay of Birsay', in *Orkney Heritage*, 2, (Birsay: A Centre of Political and Ecclesiastical Power), pp. 119–51.

Morris, C.D., Batey, C.E. and Rackham, D.J., et al. 1995. *Excavations and Survey of a Norse Settlement in Caithness*, NABO/Highland Regional Council Monograph no. 1 (New York, Glasgow and Tromsø.).

Myhre, B., 1976. 'Naustuft fra Eldre Jernalder på Stend i Fana', *Viking*, 40, pp. 29–78.

Myhre, B., 1980. 'Gardsanlegget på Ullandhaug', *Gardshus i jernalder og tidlig middelalder i Sorvest Norge*, 1, AMS Skrifter, 4, Arkeologisk Mus (Stavanger).

NMRS MS 28 a-c (SAS 461). A.O. Curle's excavation notebooks held by the National Monuments Record for Scotland, Edinburgh.

Norlund, P., 1930. 'Norse ruins at Gardar, the episcopal seat of medieval Greenland', *Meddelelser om Gronland*, 76, pp. 1–170.

Omand, D. (ed.), 1989. *The New Caithness Book* (Wick).

Quine, G., 1990. 'Upland settlement in the kingdom of Man and the Isles', unpublished PhD thesis, University of Durham.

RCAHMS 1911. Third Report. *The Inventory of Monuments and Constructions in the County of Caithness* (Edinburgh).

Richards, J.D., 1991. *Viking Age England*, English Heritage (London).

Ritchie, A., 1977. 'Excavation of Pictish and Viking-age farmsteads at Buckquoy, Orkney', *Proc Soc Antiq Scot*, 108, 1976–77, pp. 174–227.

Roussell, A., 1943a. 'Skallakot, Þjorsadalur', in *Forntida Gardar i Island*, ed. M. Stenberger (Copenhagen), pp. 55–71.

Roussell, A., 1943b. 'Stöng, Þjorsadalur', in *Forntida Gardar i Island*, ed. M. Stenberger (Copenhagen), pp. 72–97.

Small, A., 1966. 'Excavations at Underhoull, Unst, Shetland', *Proc Soc Antiq Scot*, 98, 1964–66, pp. 225–45.

Small, A., 1971. 'The Viking Highlands—A geographical view', in *The Dark Ages in the Highlands*, ed. E. Meldrum (Inverness), pp. 69–90.

Small, A. (ed.), 1965. *Fourth Viking Congress. York, August 1961*, Aberdeen University Studies 149 (Edinburgh and London).

Smith, B. (ed.) 1985. *Shetland Archaeology. New Work in Shetland in the 1970s* (Lerwick).

Stenberger, M. (ed.), 1943. *Forntida Gardar i Island* (Copenhagen).

Thorsteinsson, A., 1976. 'Testimony of ancient architecture', *Faroe Isles Review*, 1, no. 1, pp. 12–19.

CHAPTER FIVE

The Mid–Late Anglo-Saxon Period: Settlement and Land Use

Della Hooke

The mid to late Anglo-Saxon period was a period in which some regions began to experience such massive change that the characteristics they acquired have left an imprint on the landscape that has lasted to the present day, despite subsequent changes.

Perhaps one of the greatest changes experienced at this time concerned the reorganization of settlements and field systems. Although only parts of the country were affected, the resulting image of a tightly clustered village set amidst its arable fields has long been viewed as one of the most typical of English scenes—witness any collection of Christmas cards or calendars. Such a scene, with the cottages sometimes built around a village green and usually overlooked by the village church, may indeed in the later Middle Ages have been familiar in many parts of England, especially in the Midlands and the south (in Oxfordshire such villages were often more than a mile across), but was clearly not typical of many other parts of the country. The alternative, broadly speaking, was a settlement pattern made up of scattered farmsteads with, perhaps, hamlets of labourers' cottages at crossroads or alongside patches of waste. Such a pattern was often a feature of wooded or pastoral regions. In the Middle Ages, the villages were often set within the great open fields in which their inhabitants worked their scattered strip holdings, but the dispersed farms were surrounded mainly by enclosed fields.

Such a view is, of course, a gross over-simplification of what really existed but it does show the ultimate contrasts which were eventually distinguishable. This chapter is, however, concerned with the beginnings, not the eventual state, of regional differences, and even at this stage regional variation is evident.

Settlement Patterns in 'Champion' Regions

Certain regions are known to have experienced the type of reorganization that culminated in the landscape of nucleated villages and open arable fields. Much emphasis has been placed upon village planning since June Sheppard in the 1970s began to study the numerical basis for village planning in the north of England (Sheppard 1974, 1976). She stressed the opportunity for such reorganization of settlements after the 'harrying of the North' of the Norman invasions and, ever since, scholars have remained undecided about how far back deliberate village planning can be taken (Roberts 1978, 1982).

Neither settlement nucleation nor communally owned fields were necessarily totally fresh innovations of the later Anglo-Saxon period. Clustering of settlement has been a feature of rural society in Britain from a very early date, well exemplified in Cornwall, for instance, in the late Iron Age and Roman period, with settlements such as those at Chysauster. What concentration within a village does suggest, however, is a group of people working together in a communally-organized activity or, at least, with shared interests, whether these were mineral-working, fishing or farming. It is now beginning to look more and more as if the nucleation of the late Anglo-Saxon village was a way of achieving greater efficiency in agricultural production, closely linked with the development of open field agriculture.

There is now an increasing understanding of the ultimate development of such planning found in the long strip field systems of eastern England, each associated with a tightly nucleated settlement, but no precise date of origin for this particular system can yet be confidently suggested (Harvey 1983; Hall 1988). The antecedents for settlement planning, at least, may go back to the middle Anglo-Saxon period. The generally accepted model of change is that nucleation led to the abandonment of scattered early Anglo-Saxon farmsteads (Hall 1988; Taylor 1983, pp. 116–17). Such a pattern has been detected by the location of pottery sherds found by intensive fieldwalking but this method is obviously only possible in areas where pottery was generally in use—again, in eastern England. Some of the earliest settlements with signs of planning, however, seem to pre-date this phase. One might cite North Elmham in Norfolk, occupied from the late seventh century, or Wickham Bonhunt in Essex, which seems to show evidence of deliberate planning by the late sixth or early seventh century (Wade-Martins 1980; Wade 1980). It may not be coincidental that arguments can be presented to suggest that the latter was a royal vill (Bassett 1989, p. 25) and planning may have been most readily achieved on a royal or high-ranking estate. In all events, it was an exceedingly long time before the nucleated village was to become a regular component of the landscape over entire regions and, even then, site stability was by no means assured.

Nucleation is not, of course, necessarily the same as regular planning, which, in central and southern England, at least, may not have taken place in many villages until after the Norman Conquest and in many did not occur at all. Sometimes it was associated with such factors as castle building and was often, until relatively recent times, a feature associated with lordly control.

Turning to the reorganization of field systems, it is possible that reorganization of these was also at first more readily achieved on estates held by the king or by high-ranking officials. It is doubtful, however, whether fragmented holdings in communally owned arable were as much an innovation as has sometimes been thought. Doleland and common crops are already referred to in Ine's laws in late seventh-century Wessex (Attenborough 1922, pp. 48–49, Ine 42; Fox 1981, pp. 86–87). Neither does the earliest charter evidence for common arable come from a champion open field region—a reference to *gemænan land* occurs on the boundary of Cofton

Hackett in AD 849 in the woodland fringe of north-east Worcestershire where pockets of open field, however small, were an ancient component of the medieval landscape (Sawyer 1968, S 1272; Hooke 1988a). There are many forms of tenurial arrangements which display some degree of common ownership and the temporary right of an individual to work a particular plot of land. Beyond England, it seems likely from the evidence contained in Welsh law codes that the Welsh *maerdref* operated on a similar system of land allotment, with strips worked by inhabitants living under a particularly servile kind of tenure because it was their collective responsibility to maintain the vill for the visits of the king and his retinue when he toured the *commotes* of his kingdom. Although the written manuscripts date only from the thirteenth century it is believed that they embody much earlier material (Jones 1972, pp. 284–85).

Few would dispute, however, that major changes occurred in the later Anglo-Saxon period. One has only to look at events this century to see how rapidly collectivization under a strong central authority can transform both field and settlement patterns. To a struggling peasantry striving to eke a living from the land at the subsistence levels which seem to have operated in post-Roman Britain, such a sharing of labour resources might even have seemed an attractive venture if they were indeed allotted shares in the land in proportion to their holdings. In the charters of the tenth and eleventh centuries the division of resources seldom seems to have been between many tenants, such as *se fifta æcer þære dal mædue*, 'the fifth acre of the partible meadow', which belonged to the hide of land at Himbleton, Worcestershire, in the later tenth century (Sawyer 1968, S 1373). Here, however, we may be seeing division between lessees of manors rather than the peasants themselves. The phraseology of the mid-tenth-century charter relating to Avon in Durnsford, Wiltshire, sounds much more like the state of affairs in the medieval open field: *singulis iugeribus mixtum in communi rure huc illacque dispersis*, 'single acres dispersed in a mixture here and there in common land' (Sawyer 1968, S 719), while at Charlton, Berkshire, in AD 982, the five hides granted by King Æthelred to his *minister*, Ælfgar, were 'not demarcated on all sides by clear bounds because to left and right lie acres in combination one with another': *rus namque prætaxatum manifestis indique terminis minus diuiditur, quia iugera altrinsecus copulata adiacent* (Sawyer 1968, S 839; Finberg 1972, p. 490).

The aim of bringing the farmers into a central settlement seems to have been the achievement of greater efficiency, able, too, to produce a surplus of agricultural commodities. Such a move could arise from a variety of causes: pressure of population has been a popular suggestion in recent writings, particularly where there had been an extension of the arable land. Thirsk (1964, 1966) has seen the necessity to control common grazing of waste and harvest stubble as an important contributory factor once population increase and extension of the arable had led to a shortage of pasture for domestic stock, including plough oxen; others (Bishop 1938) have stressed the sharing of land between those who had cleared it, and recently Higham has suggested that the number of plough oxen could be kept to a minimum if farms were located in a central village (Higham 1989).

Reorganization, in Midland and south-central England at least, appears to have taken place within the individual township unit, the forerunner of the Domesday manor (Fig. 5.1) (Fox 1981). This, in itself, indicates that it came into effect with the fragmentation of larger estates which is so clearly evident in pre-Conquest charters. In such circumstances, the motive behind reorganization might be the wish to improve the efficiency and revenues of the recently established individual manor (Dodgshon 1980). Until the seventh century, at least, it is doubtful whether Anglo-Saxon England had a middle tier of society sufficiently widely and well established to fill the role of landed thegn. The kingdoms themselves were only becoming established in the sixth century and many of the earliest land grants to either the church or to a lay populace involved tracts of land considerably more extensive than the township estate. It is only by about the late ninth century that these smaller units begin to figure so prominently in charter grants.

By the tenth and eleventh centuries in many regions these units can be seen to be becoming increasingly independent of the capital manor, shown particularly clearly, for instance, in the fine series of

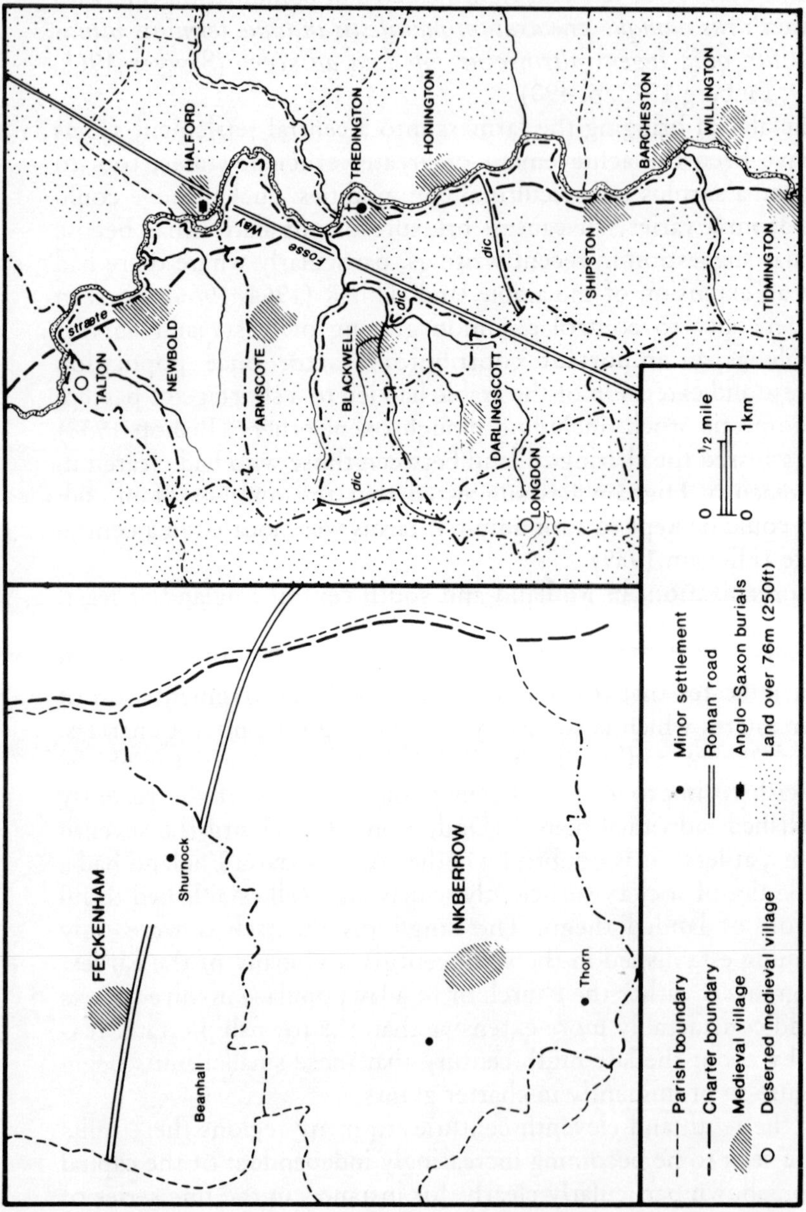

Fig. 5.1 Early medieval estates and parishes: (a) in a woodland region of Worcestershire (b) in a valley region of south Warwickshire.

leases made by the Church of Worcester within the Hwiccan kingdom. At Tredington, now in Warwickshire (Fig. 5.1), the estate apparently took its name from an eighth-century *comes*, Tyrdda, who held it before the under-kings of the Hwicce granted it to the Bishop of Worcester (Sawyer 1968, S 55). Although the Church of Worcester kept the main part of its estate here together in a single large ecclesiastical parish, parts of it were set aside for the maintenance of the monks and separately assessed in Domesday Book; other townships within the parish were leased out to various thegns at intervals.

By the later Anglo-Saxon period, references in charters to the boundaries of neighbouring communities clearly show that a dense network of minor boundaries had come into being, sometimes more than have survived to the present day (Hooke 1981, pp. 100–6). There is evidence that the desired self-sufficiency of the individual manor often led to detached parcels of land being added to a particular estate. In Old Stratford, Warwickshire, an estate at Bishopton (Sawyer 1968, S 1388) in AD 1016 was allotted 8½ acres of meadowland on Shottery water-meadow, another 15 acres 'opposite Tiddington', 12 acres of ploughland and Ælfric's wood, all of which seem to have come from within a pre-existing multiple estate held by the Bishop of Worcester since at least the early ninth century (Hooke 1988a).

The most regular pattern of subdivision seems to have been achieved in some valley areas of southern England, particularly in the chalklands. Here, there was obviously an attempt to include different types of land within each township: a pattern of valley meadows, arable land on the slopes of the downland, and pasture on the higher land, can be identified from charter evidence, the pasture apparently making use of marginal land no longer required for agriculture (Hooke 1988b). There were often a number of linear townships within the ecclesiastical parish and in the post-medieval period even the manorial demesne can be identified as a separate linear unit. Within these units, the medieval settlement nucleus frequently lay at the foot of the escarpment close to the township arable but by then could vary in size from a village to a mere isolated farm. Uffington, outside this pattern, may have been a deliberate foundation by Abingdon Abbey. Sometimes two original nuclei seem to have fused to form a larger settlement. In the Vale of the White Horse in Oxfordshire one such fusion seems to have occurred in the mid-tenth century when a thegn succeeded in acquiring two adjacent estates, the village then taking his name 'Wulfric's *tūn*', now Woolstone (Gelling 1976, p. 677).

Settlement nucleation does not, however, seem to have occurred quickly and may have been an ongoing process for several centuries in many areas. In one of the classic 'champion' areas, the Vale of Evesham in Worcestershire, the villages may have come into being by the tenth century but charter boundary clauses of late Anglo-Saxon date refer to a number of additional settlements beside boundaries, none of which survived into the post-medieval period (Hooke 1985). In Wormleighton, in the Warwickshire Feldon, another classic region of settlement nucleation, Domesday folios record sub-tenancies which might be indicative of separate settlement nuclei, no fewer than six being noted for the period immediately prior to the Norman Conquest (Hooke 1989). Higham (1989) has further suggested that where plough teams outnumber ploughlands in the Domesday folios these were probably kept on outlying farms. If so, large sections of Warwickshire still maintained a settlement pattern that was far from nucleated in 1086, both within and beyond the regions later characterized by nucleation. Tenth-century charters also suggest that some enclosed land lay beyond the open fields in the later Anglo-Saxon period, although it was to be incorporated into the latter by medieval times.

There is, unfortunately, little charter evidence for eastern England, the area of ultimate replanning. A Yorkshire charter for Newbold refers to lands lying in 'every other acre' in the tenth century and another for Normanton in Nottinghamshire to 'every third acre' in the same century (Sawyer 1968, S 716, S 659). The twelfth-century *Liber Eliensis*, using evidence from earlier vernacular documents, also suggests that subdivided arable (here 'every eighth acre') was present at Brandon in the Suffolk Breckland (*Liber Eliensis*, ed. Blake 1962, p. 111). The charter evidence, at least, confirms that open field agriculture had been established here but as yet there is little hard dating evidence for the long strips which extended from the village core to the boundaries of the land unit.

Evidence of regular subdivision has been archaeologically attested at West Cotton in Raunds, Northamptonshire, but at present has not been tied to individual building plots (MSRG 1987) but to a late Saxon timbered building. We are, then, still left with something of a 'black hole' for the earliest indications of change but we can also be sure that this took place in different areas at very different times and to varying degrees.

Areas of Dispersed Settlement

A contrasting regional type is that which remained unaffected to any marked degree by the type of reorganization outlined above. In so far as dispersed settlement seems to have been the dominant pattern of the Romano-British rural landscape, this may be seen as a more ancient form. Certainly there is some evidence to suggest that some early Anglo-Saxon farmsteads were squeezed into a pre-existing landscape of individual farmsteads at Catholme in Staffordshire or near Abingdon in Oxfordshire (Esmonde Cleary 1989, pp. 196–99; Losco-Bradley 1977; Miles 1984), and where pottery evidence has been preserved, as over much of eastern England, early and middle Anglo-Saxon farmsteads remained dispersed, as previously noted. There must have been many different scenarios across Britain but it is doubtful if the difference between regions was as marked in the later Anglo-Saxon period as in subsequent periods. More probably, the differences were again ones of degree.

A pattern characterized by few villages but largely made up of dispersed farmsteads and hamlets is characteristic of large areas of England, even today. Many such areas were ones of lower population density throughout medieval times, usually in wooded or pastoral regions where arable farming was initially less important. The Arden area of Warwickshire presents a classic example of such a region: amply supplied with woodland and waste, the region may initially have been linked with more developed regions, such as the Feldon in the south of the county, for the seasonal exploitation of its wood-pasture and for its other woodland resources. It appears to have been a region of scattered settlement by late Anglo-Saxon times (Hooke 1985, pp. 173–80). Further colonization in the twelfth and thirteenth centuries merely perpetuated the dispersed nature of its settlement pattern, resulting in the establishment of individual farmsteads rapidly consolidating their holdings around them, with the demise of much of the early open field (Roberts 1968). This is not to say that open field was entirely absent, however. Even in the heart of the Arden region, where waste remained plentiful, it was present in association with what seem to have been tiny manorial nuclei, later, where it survived, giving rise to the typical 'woodland field system' characterized by numerous small patches of open field scattered throughout a parish area (Roberts 1973). Here, too, there is early evidence of individual settlements bearing *worð* or *wīc* names, some of the latter herding establishments.

Not all such areas were ones of sparse population and in Essex Williamson has argued that the dispersed pattern was perpetuated largely for social reasons. Here rapid conquest by semi-autonomous groups may have led to the survival of 'extended kindreds as a prime force in land-holding' (Williamson 1988), with a measure of freedom surviving amongst the peasantry which permitted them to congregate around commons and greens to a much greater extent than elsewhere and to avoid the reorganization experienced elsewhere.

The west of Britain also seems to be an area in which scattered farmsteads are a long-established component of the settlement pattern, but one must be aware of the danger of interpreting early patterns upon the basis of familiarity with the present landscape. There may not have been a great deal of difference between a family farmstead with numerous retainers and a small manorial hamlet with only a few peasants. What differences in tenure there were, however, we can still only guess at. Moreover, a single farmstead which today looks as if it has survived unaltered for centuries may hide many changes which have left little mark upon the present-day landscape. As a salutary example of the latter, the royal *maerdref* of Ystumgwern lay on the coast of Merioneth in Gwynedd, Wales. Ystumgwern was the royal hamlet of the *commote* of Ardudwy Is Artro, its members tied by bond tenure. In this area the rocky hills of the Rhinog range rise quickly from the coast and centuries of cultivation are squeezed onto the same narrow strip of coastal land. Only recently, Colin Gresham (1988) succeeded in identifying the location of the *maerdref* and found that it had been replaced by only two or three Tudor farms. Four of the bond holdings had been given to villein families displaced by the building of Edward I's borough at Harlech, these four having been replaced by the modern holding of Faildref, while the remainder of the demesne land, supporting in total some twenty holdings, lay adjacent. This may be the reason why one of the neighbouring farms, Taltreuddyn, was entered as a township of thirteen households in 1293 (Thomas 1970, p. 130, n. 5). Here, therefore, a small handful of later farms has replaced an earlier settlement cluster.

If the dominant land use of such areas was pastoralism, and there was an abundance of woodland and waste, there would be little incentive for massive reorganization of either settlement or field systems. Certainly estate fragmentation took place but it was often transitory in nature and subdivision may not always have been absolute. Within the large parish of Inkberrow in Worcestershire, the inhabitants of the hamlet of Thorne held shares in the arable lands and common copse of Inkberrow in the mid-tenth century (Sawyer 1968, S 1305) (Fig. 5.1). On the margins of the Forest of Feckenham, such small communities as Thorne were too lacking in resources to support their own church and to form a separate ecclesiastical parish so that early minor boundaries remain difficult to trace today.

Much of the south-west peninsula seems to have been an area of both scattered settlements and tiny village nuclei but at present the archaeological record is still incomplete. The network of settlements present by the time of the Norman Conquest is often masked by the nature of the Domesday entries, with many individual settlements assessed together under the name of a capital manor. Where central estate control had been relaxed, however, one often gets glimpses of a full and active countryside.

The area which lay to the south of Crediton Hundred provides one such example, with numerous Domesday manors which in 1066 had been held separately even when within the lands of one landowner (Fig. 5.2). This is the land which had been claimed by Crediton minster but which failed to remain within its territory (Hooke forthcoming). In the south, Drewsteignton was obviously dominant, with land for twelve ploughs on the two-hide manor, eight teams working, and a recorded population of twenty-four individuals, but the later parish included six other Domesday vills, all of them single-virgate holdings. On these manors the number of plough teams recorded was less than the number of ploughlands and, if we are to take this at face value, it may mean that the land was felt to be capable of further development. In this area of broken topography, sheep greatly outnumbered cattle on the demesne land. Woodland is not greatly in evidence in the Domesday recordings, only noted to any extent on the sheriff's manor of Hittisleigh where it measured '1 league long and ½ league wide' (Thorn and Thorn 1985, 16, 114). Today most of the surviving woodland is confined to the narrow valleys of deeply incised streams draining northwards into the Yeo but it was obviously more extensive in the past.

The great Crediton charter boundary (Sawyer 1968, S 255) gives us few details of the settlements of the area but does enable us to trace the bounds of the estate rather more closely than many have believed. It also names the topographical features of the countryside which were seen as boundary markers. Not surprisingly, coombs are often mentioned, especially in the south of the area, although the open nature of *swincumb*, 'the coomb of swine', on the western boundary of Colebrooke, suggests that the *cumbe* term was used rather loosely in Devon. Hills and ridges are noted and the several references to a *hlȳp*, 'a leap', may be to a narrow gorge-like valley. There is one where the boundary crosses an incised stream near Hook Farm on the northern boundary of Cheriton Bishop and another near Woolfardisworthy on the northern

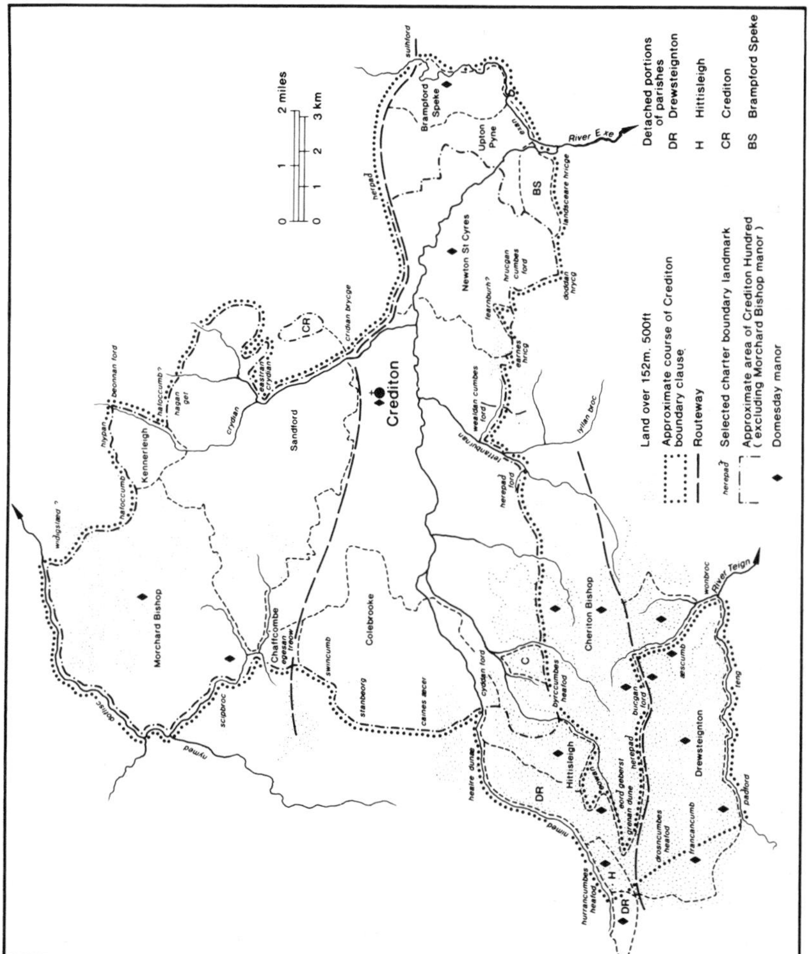

Fig. 5.2 The estates of Crediton Minster, Devon.

boundary of Kennerleigh. It is obviously only when the charter boundary clauses have been solved as closely as possible that it becomes realistic to try to trace these features on the ground.

In many instances, the boundary clauses enable one to trace at least some of the major routeways which made their way across the peninsula. A *herepað*, a 'highway' route, for instance, may be traced across the Crediton estate to Creedy Bridge, at one point on the Sandford boundary overlooked by a hill described as a *weard setl*, 'a look-out' or 'watch place'. To the east of Creedy Bridge a branch ran south-eastwards and followed the southern boundary of Shobrooke before crossing the Exe at *sulhford* at the north-western corner of Stoke Canon and then the Culm at the 'long ford', the latter probably at Columbjohn. Fords were frequently referred to in the Devon charters and were much commoner than bridges. One can similarly trace a number of the routeways which ran seawards across the South Hams, often following the ridges. One of the major bridges, Kingsbridge, is recorded in a grant of Sorley in AD 962 (Sawyer 1968, S 704; Hooke 1990; 1994, pp. 165–68) and the same charter refers to an earthwork apparently on the site of the present town, suggesting that a fortified burh had indeed been established by this date (Haslam 1984).

Cornish charters reveal a similar pattern of tiny settlement nuclei, often naming settlements other than those recorded in 1086. On the Lizard peninsula, a large monastic estate was apparently being broken up in the tenth century and granted into secular ownership. A number of boundary clauses relate to the holdings of Lesneage, Pennare, Traboe, Trevallack and Grugwith in St Keverne and to Trethewey in St Martin-in-Meneage (Sawyer 1968, S 755, S 832) but Domesday Book also mentions the manors of Roscarnon, Trenance, Trelan and Trembraze which seem to have lain within St Keverne parish.

There are enormous differences between the Cornish and Devon evidence, however, arising out of the late conquest of Cornwall by the Anglo-Saxons. These will be outlined in a forthcoming paper and can only be mentioned briefly here. Basically, there is the delight of having the landscape described by those who actually saw it at the time in their own speech. In Cornwall, this means in the Cornish tongue. Instead of the Devon tors, we find references to such features as *carn winnioc*, 'the white tor', on the boundary of Trenowth or *carn peran*, 'Piran's tor', on the north-eastern boundary of Perranzabuloe. Archaeological features include two rounds on the boundaries of Trenowth and Tregellas, 'the witch's round' and 'the wide round', described by the Cornish term *ker*; a stone row on the southern boundary of Trerice; and various barrows such as those on the boundary of Grugwith (which may be a reference to the cist known as the 'Three Brothers of Grugith'—Ordnance Survey Crugith—on Crousa Downs), or others on the eastern boundary of Perranzabuloe.

Since most of the Cornish charters are late in date, it may not be surprising that there are references to mills, noted at St Buryan and Tinnel as well as at Trerice (Sawyer 1968, S 450, S 951). As in all boundary clauses, references to settlements are few, largely because these were usually well within the boundaries, but in Devon a number of *worð* features named are probably farmsteads. These include *burhgeardes worðig* on the boundary of Culmstock, two *weorðig* features to the east of the Creedy mentioned in a Sandford boundary clause (Sawyer 1968, S 386, S 405, S 998), and *ellewurðie* on the coastal downs above Budleigh Salterton. Many of the boundary settlements in charter boundary clauses are named by use of the habitative term *worð*, literally 'enclosure', which seems to have denoted a single enclosed farmstead (Hooke 1989, p. 25).

Since the main subject of this essay has been settlements and field systems, it may be fitting to end with the very brief allusions to the latter recorded in the charters of the south-west. These are found as additions to the boundary clauses, also written in Old English. Finberg drew attention to the charter of Ayshford and Boehill in Devon, granting 2½ *mansæ* and 25 *segetes* to Eadheah in AD 958, which notes *þonon is her butan þam gemæne les stræt. þonon synt þær manega hylla þæ man erien mæg*, 'then here outside the common pasture is (the) street, whence there are many hills which one may plough', suggesting that such land might be taken in if necessary from time to time (Sawyer 1968, S 653; Finberg 1972, p. 494). This seems to show a typical infield/outfield arrangement in which some of the outlying land belonging to a manor, perhaps normally used as common pasture, might be taken into cultivation from time to time as necessary. Also referring clearly to common ownership is the reference in the grant of half a yardland at Trerice in St Dennis to Eadulf in AD 1049 (Sawyer 1968, S 1019) which adds *7 beon* þ*a þorðigas. 7* þ*[a] bereland. 7 seo myln. 7 se ut hlȳp gemæne*, 'and the enclosures (farmsteads), and the barley land, and the mill and the out-leap are common'. Today fossilized strip fields are present in this township and subdivided holdings may have been present in central Cornwall by the eleventh century (Hooke and Herring 1993).

The Trerice charter also notes that the *ut hlȳp*, the outlying pasture, was held in common. By this date estate fragmentation had led communities to seek this resource close at hand but both charters and place-names show that rights in more distant grazings had not been entirely lost. *Peadingtun*, a large estate on the open moorland of Dartmoor to the north of Ashburton which possesses an updated boundary clause (Sawyer 1968, S 1547), has been identified by Fox (forthcoming) as the moorland manor of Paignton, a coastal manor of the Bishop of Exeter. Domesday Book shows similar linkages between coastal manors and their moorland holdings: the Domesday manor of 'Dewdon', for instance, was probably Jordan in Widecombe-in-the-Moor which was a dependent manor of Cockington on Tor Bay (Thorn and Thorn 1985, 20, 10). Summer shielings on the moor probably served these seasonal pastures before they gave way to more permanent settlement.

The landscapes of the south-west, so often regarded as some of the oldest in England, may well include features which are genuinely ancient but they also contain indisputable evidence of having been affected by the changes which characterized so much of the country in the early medieval period.

There can be little doubt that the period between the end of Roman Britain and the Norman Conquest was one of the most formative of English history. Further perusal of the documents still gives rise to fresh interpretation of the written evidence and additional sources of evidence such as place-names help to fill out the written record. Slowly archaeology, in all its facets, will provide new data that will add to our knowledge of settlement patterns and related land use. The most precious source of evidence remains the landscape itself, both the hidden below-ground landscape detectable only by excavation, cropmark analysis and techniques of surface archaeology, and the visible one of settlements, fields and enclosures. Techniques for unravelling the latter are still being developed and have by no means been exhausted: a continued multidisciplinary approach can still provide fresh information and new ideas.

References

Attenborough, F.L., 1922. *The Laws of the Earliest English Kings* (Cambridge).

Bassett, S., 1989. 'In search of the origins of Anglo-Saxon kingdoms', in *The Origins of Anglo-Saxon Kingdoms*, ed. S. Bassett (Leicester).

Birch, W. de Gray, 1885–99. *Cartularium Saxonicum*, 3 vols (no place).

Bishop, T.A.M., 1938 'Assarting and the growth of the open fields', *Economic History Review*, 1st ser, 6, no. 1, pp. 13–29.

Dodgshon, R.A., 1980. *The Origins of British Field Systems: An Interpretation* (London).

Esmonde Cleary, A.S., 1989. *The Ending of Roman Britain* (London).

Finberg, H.P.R., 1972. 'Anglo-Saxon England to 1042', in *The Agrarian History of England and Wales, AD 43–1042*, ed. H.P.R. Finberg (Cambridge).

Fox, H.S.A., 1981. 'Approaches to the adoption of the Midland system', in *The Origins of Open-Field Agriculture*, ed. T. Rowley (London), pp. 64–111.

Fox, H.S.A., forthcoming. 'The bounds of Paignton on Dartmoor; a new identification of an Old English boundary perambulation of *circa* 1050' (no place).

Gelling, G., 1976. *The Place-Names of Berkshire, Part III*, English Place-Name Society, 51 (Cambridge).

Gresham, C., 1987/88. 'Addendum: "Vairdre alias Vaildre"', *J Merioneth Hist & Record Soc*, 10, Pt 3, pp. 221–26.

Hall, D., 1988. 'The late Saxon countryside: villages and their fields', in *Anglo-Saxon Settlements*, ed. D. Hooke (Oxford), pp. 99–122.

Harvey, M., 1983. 'Planned field systems in eastern Yorkshire: some thoughts on their origin', *Agricultural History Review*, 31, pp. 91–103.

Haslam, J., 1984. 'The towns of Devon', in *Anglo-Saxon Towns in Southern England*, ed. J. Haslam (Chichester), pp. 249–83.

Higham, N., 1989. 'Settlement, land use and Domesday ploughlands', *Landscape History*, 12, pp. 3–43.

Hooke, D., 1981. *Anglo-Saxon Landscapes of the West Midlands: The Charter Evidence*, Br Archaeol Rep, Br Ser, 95 (Oxford).

Hooke, D., 1985. 'Village development in the West Midlands', in *Medieval Villages, a Review of Current Work*, ed. D. Hooke, Oxford University Committee of Archaeology Monograph 5 (Oxford), pp. 125–54.

Hooke, D., 1988a. 'Early forms of open-field agriculture in England', *Geografiska Annaler*, 70 B (1), pp. 123–31.

Hooke, D., 1988b. 'Regional variation in southern and central England in the Anglo-Saxon period and its relationship to land units and settlement', in *Anglo-Saxon Settlements*, ed. D. Hooke (Oxford), pp. 123–51.

Hooke, D., 1989. 'Early medieval estate and settlement patterns: the documentary evidence', in *The Rural Settlements of Medieval England*, ed. M. Aston, D. Austin and C. Dyer (Oxford), pp. 9–30.

Hooke, D., 1990. 'Studies on Devon charter boundaries', *Rep Trans Devon Assoc Advmt Sci*, 122, pp. 193–211.

Hooke, D., forthcoming. 'Saxon conquest and settlement', in *An Historical Atlas of South-West England*, ed. R.J.P. Kain and W. Ravenhill (Exeter).

Hooke, D., 1992. 'Charters and the landscape', *Nomina*, 15 (1991–92), pp. 75–96.

Hooke, D., and Herring, P., 1993, 'Interrogating Anglo-Saxons in St Dennis', *Cornish Archaeology*, 32, pp. 67–75.

Jones, G.R.J., 1972. 'Post-Roman Wales', in *The Agrarian History of England and Wales, AD 43–1042*, ed. H.P.R. Finberg (Cambridge), pp. 283–382.

Kemble, J.M., 1839–48. *Codex Diplomaticus Aevi Saxonici*, 6 vols (no place).

Losco-Bradley, S., 1977. 'Catholme', *Current Archaeology*, 59, pp. 358–64.

MSRG (Medieval Settlement Research Group), 1987. *Annual Report*, 2.

Miles, D., 1984. *Archaeology at Barton Court Farm, Abingdon, Oxon.*, Counc Br Archaeol, Res Rep 50 (London).

Roberts, B.K., 1968. 'A study of medieval colonization in the Forest of Arden, Warwickshire', *Agricultural History Review*, 16, pp. 101–13.

Roberts, B.K., 1973. 'Field systems of the West Midlands', in *Studies of Field Systems in the British Isles*, ed. A.R.H. Baker and R.A. Butlin (Cambridge), pp. 188–231.

Roberts, B.K., 1978. 'The regulated village in northern England: some problems and questions', *Geographica Polonica*, 38, pp. 245–52.
Roberts, B.K., 1982. *Village Plans* (Aylesbury).
Rose-Troup, F., 1929, 'The new Edgar charter and the South Hams', *Rep Trans Devon Assoc Advmt Sci*, 61, pp. 249–80.
Sawyer, P.H., 1968. *Anglo-Saxon Charters, an Annotated List and Bibliography*, Royal Hist Soc (London).
Sheppard, J., 1974. 'Metrological analysis of regular village plans in Yorkshire', *Agricultural History Review*, 22, pp. 118–35.
Sheppard, J., 1976. 'Medieval village planning in northern England: some evidence from Yorkshire', *Journal of Historical Geography*, 2, pp. 3–20.
Taylor, C., 1983. *Village and Farmstead* (London).
Thirsk, J., 1964. 'The common fields', *Past and Present*, 29, pp. 3–25.
Thirsk, J., 1966. 'The origin of the common fields', *Past and Present*, 33, pp. 142–47.
Thomas, C., 1970. 'Social organisation and rural settlement in medieval North Wales', *J Merioneth Hist & Rec Soc*, 6, pt 2, pp. 121–31.
Thorn, C., and Thorn, F., 1985. *Domesday Book, 9, Devon* (Chichester).
Wade, K., 1980. 'A settlement site at Wickham Bonhunt, Essex', in *Archaeology in Essex to AD 1500*, ed. D.G. Buckley, Counc Br Archaeol, Res Rep 34, pp. 96–102.
Wade-Martins, P., 1980. 'Excavation in North Elmham Park 1967–72', *East Anglian Archaeology*, 9, pp. 1–661.
Williamson, T., 1988. 'Explaining regional landscapes: woodland and champion in southern and eastern England', *Landscape History*, 10, pp. 5–13.

Published and manuscript sources for the pre-Conquest charters cited (in order of occurrence). Fresh transcripts of the pre-Conquest charters of Devon and Cornwall, with accompanying solutions of the boundary clauses, are to be found in Hooke, D., 1994. *Pre-Conquest Charter-Bounds of Devon and Cornwall* (Woodbridge).

S 1272, Birch 1885–99, B 455 (1); B.L., Cotton Tiberius, A.xiii, fos 3r–4r.
S 1373, Kemble 1839–48, K 680; B.L., Cotton Tiberius, A.xiii, fo. 72r/v.
S 719, Birch 1885–99, B 1120; B.L., Harley 436, fos 64v–66v.
S 839, Kemble 1839–48, K 1278; B.L., Cotton Claudius, B.vi, fos 93v–94r.
S 55, Birch 1885–99, B 183; B.L., Cotton Tiberius, A.xiii, fos 16r–17v.
S 1388, Somers charter 19, in Smith, J., 1722. *Historia Ecclesiastica Gentis Anglorum* (Cambridge).

S 716, Birch 1885–99, B 1113; York, Dean and Chapter, *Magnum Registrum Album*, Pt 1, fo. 57r/v.

S 1305, Birch 1885–99, B 1110; B.L., Cotton Tiberius, A.xiii, fos 88r–89r.

S 255, Birch 1885–99, B 1331; Oxford, Bodleian, Eng. hist. a.2, no. 1.

S 704, Rose-Troup 1929, pp. 250–51; Chelmsford, Essex Record Office, D/DP T 209.

S 755, Birch 1885–99, B 1197, Exeter, Dean and Chapter, 2521 (pr. *Facsimiles of Anglo-Saxon Manuscripts*, ed. W.B. Sanders, Ordnance Survey, Southampton, 1878–84, II, Exeter 6).

S 832, Exeter, Dean and Chapter, 2527v (pr. *Facsimiles*, ibid., II, Exeter 14 dorse).

S 386, Birch 1885–99, B 724; Exeter, Dean and Chapter, 2519 (pr. *Facsimiles*, ibid., II, Exeter 2).

S 405, Birch 1885–99, B 1343, Oxford, Bodleian, Eng. hist. a. 2, no. III.

S 998, Kemble 1839–48, K 1332; B.L., Additional, 46487, fos 29r–30r.

S 653, Birch 1885–99, B 1027; B.L., Additional, 15350, fo. 67v.

S 1019, Canterbury, Dean and Chapter, *Chartae Antiquae* C 1281 (pr. *Facsimiles*. I.24).

CHAPTER SIX

Settlement, Land Use and Estate Patterns on the Failand Ridge, North Somerset: A Preliminary Discussion

C.J. Bond

Introduction

Man's perception of his past and present relationship with his environment is an ever-changing one. The doctrine of environmental determinism, the idea that the siting of human settlement and the patterns of land exploitation were largely dictated by physiographic factors such as geology, soil, relief and drainage, first developed by Continental scholars such as Ratzel and Leplay, was introduced to the English-speaking world earlier this century by the American geographer Ellen Churchill Semple. This view retained some influence as late as the 1950s, though most archaeologists and landscape historians had discarded it in its most extreme form long before. It was generally superseded by a more anthropocentric approach, not far removed from the theory of possibilism expressed by Febvre in the 1920s, which placed more emphasis upon the role of human decision-making—'there are no necessities, only possibilities, and man, as master of the possibilities, is judge of their use' (for a summary of this debate see Tatham 1957). This in turn led on to a range of models derived from economics and other social sciences, in which the natural environment was perceived as a negative factor, something to be controlled and exploited through technological progress. However, in the face of the world population explosion, the conspicuous consumption of the western world and the unprecedented scale and speed of modern development, many now believe that man's technological capacity has run out of control, and is no longer acting towards his long-term advantage. Current interests in organic farming and the sustainable management of resources reflect a renewed concern for balance in the relationship between man and his environment.

No-one would want a return to the outmoded dictates of old-fashioned determinism in historical and archaeological studies; nonetheless, the current practice of studying occupation sites within their landscape context and the concern with territories as a basis for assessing the resources available to communities does reflect contemporary preoccupation with environmental matters.

Many of the traditional models of land use, such as Von Thünen's 'Isolated State' concept, have consciously ignored environmental factors to concentrate upon the principles of maximizing convenience and profits while minimizing effort and costs. In a self-sufficient settlement in a featureless plain of uniform fertility, those activities involving the most intensive labour by the greatest number of people might be expected to take place closest to the settlement, those requiring less attention being relegated to a greater distance (Von Thünen 1826; for a convenient English summary, see Chisholm 1962, pp. 21–35). When Von Thünen was writing, contemporary economic conditions in his home region of eastern Germany placed a higher premium upon silviculture than would perhaps normally be the case. An adjusted version of his model would place horticultural and dairying activities close to the settlement, arable land beyond that, pastoral forms of farming at a greater distance and woodland at the perimeter of the settlement's territory. In practice, of course, few settlements ever developed such a well-marked annular pattern of land use, and one of the many factors which needs to be taken into account in attempting to explain deviations from the idealized model is the range of opportunities and constraints presented by the variations of natural topography, and the ways in which these are perceived in different periods.

The landscape of north and central Somerset, with its marked alternation of plateaux, ridges and low-lying flat land, offers particular opportunities for the study of the changing human response to a relatively extreme range of environments within a restricted compass. The following discussion will explore, as an example, the patterns of settlement and land exploitation along the Failand ridge and the lowlands on either side of it. This range of hills extends westwards from the Avon Gorge, on the outskirts of Bristol, for some 18 km, reaching the Bristol Channel coast at Clevedon. At their eastern extremity the hills form a dissected plateau some 4–5 km wide between Long Ashton and Easton-in-Gordano. They achieve their greatest elevation of 160 m above sea level in the centre, just west of Failand. Between Tickenham and the coast the hills contract to a single, narrow, steep-sided ridge. Geologically they are an offshoot of the Mendip Hills, made up mainly of Carboniferous Limestone with some Old Red Sandstone and Coal Measures thrust up through the Triassic beds which form the lowlands on either side. To the north lies the Gordano valley (this exotic-sounding name is no more than the familiar Old English *gar-denu*, 'triangular or wedge-shaped valley', which perfectly describes its character), broadening from the south-west to a width of about 2km.[1] This is closed off from the Bristol Channel by another ridge of similar geological character extending along the coast from Clevedon to Portishead. To the south is a wider expanse of low-lying moors, part of the North Somerset Levels, broken only by the low island of Coal Measures at Nailsea, and terminated by the Backwell-Congresbury ridge to the east and the main bulk of the Mendip Hills to the south. Estuarine alluvium makes up the coastal part both of the Gordano valley and of the moors to the south, while the more inland parts are largely based upon deposits of peat.

1 *Editor's note*: for Gordano, Mills prefers a derivation from Old English *gor*, hence 'dirty, muddy valley' (see Mills, AD, 1991. *A Dictionary of English Place-Names* (Oxford) p. 81. Bond agrees that this would also suit the character of the valley.

This small region has been chosen for examination for no better reason than that the author came to live in one of the villages on the southern flank of the ridge a few years ago, and has developed a personal interest in its archaeology and history. Although much valuable preliminary work has been achieved within the region by individuals and members of local archaeological and historical societies, there has as yet been no co-ordinated policy of intensive planned archaeological and documentary research. The problems of attempting to understand settlement evolution in even a single parish have been described most graphically in one recent publication where, after twenty years' work, one of the most experienced and respected field archaeologists in England was forced to admit that 'No clear picture of the origin and development of the village has emerged and indeed from the heady days when all seemed obvious, little has been achieved except a slow descent into confusion' (Taylor 1989). In the face of this chastening example, it would be folly to suggest that the current views of settlement along the Failand ridge are any more than provisional impressions, which will inevitably be modified as work progresses and more data accumulates. However, since the alternative is to give up and vegetate, some interim assessment still seems worthwhile.

The period which is the theme of the present volume, AD 400–1066, is still generally perceived as one of special difficulty in settlement studies, despite the considerable advances in understanding which have been made recently in some parts of the country (see, for example, Faull 1984; Hooke 1988). The quantity of documentation is slight compared with later periods, and its interpretation is often problematical. The archaeological evidence is equally slight and difficult to interpret; in particular the largely aceramic post-Roman cultures of many parts of western Britain, together with the extent of permanent pasture remaining in the modern landscape, tend to make fieldwork a relatively unrewarding exercise. While it seems fairly clear that significant changes were taking place in the form and location of settlement along the Failand ridge between the end of Roman administration and the Norman Conquest, the precise nature and chronology of those changes remains obscure, and to have any hope even of asking the right questions, let alone answering them, it is necessary to consider a much broader time-span, looking backwards into prehistory and forwards into the early modern period. Four basic questions may be posed:

(i) What was the nature of the local Romano-British settlement pattern, and for how long did it survive into the post-Roman period?
(ii) To what extent did the pre-Roman pattern of settlement reassert itself after the withdrawal of the central imperial government?
(iii) When and in what circumstances did the pattern of villages, hamlets and farmsteads which can be identified in the later Middle Ages first begin to take shape?
(iv) To what extent were the changes in settlement reflected by broader changes in territorial boundaries and land use?

Late Prehistoric Settlement

Even on the basis of the present limited evidence, it seems likely that much of the primeval woodland along the ridge top and lower slopes had been cleared and the landscape well settled by the end of the Bronze Age. Neolithic activity is indicated by several flint scatters on the broader part of the plateau, while more stone axes have come from the Failand ridge than from any other part of north Somerset, saving only the uplands around Bath (Darvill 1987, Map 2.10). Bronze Age material has also been found on various parts of the ridge, including some prestigious metal items such as the Clevedon gold torque and the Wraxall bronze collar (Dobson 1931, pp. 124–25). A Late Bronze Age spearhead from Cadbury in Tickenham may point to some form of occupation before the construction of the Iron Age hillfort there (Dawkins 1906, p. 192). In contrast, by comparison with the Mendip Hills, or even with the nearby Backwell plateau, very few barrows are known anywhere on the Failand ridge (Grinsell 1971). One example excavated at Court

Hill, Tickenham, contained burials dated by radio-carbon to 1375 ± 100 and 715 ± 130 bc (Green, 1973). Another Early Bronze Age crouched inhumation was subsequently discovered some 150 m to the south-west (Anderson et al. 1989). Other descriptions of barrows and megalithic features in the older literature are unreliable.

The evidence for the later prehistoric period is fuller (Fig 6.1). The focal points of settlement during the Iron Age were several hillforts along the top of the ridge. The largest is the bivallate Stokeleigh Camp, occupying 3 hectares on the western side of the Avon Gorge. Immediately to the south, on the opposite side of Nightingale Valley, is the badly-damaged site of Burwalls, a trivallate promontory fort of about 2.6 hectares, while a third hillfort lies on the eastern side of the Avon Gorge at Clifton (Atkinson, 1868–69; Scarth 1873; Morgan 1900, 1901; Haldane 1965–66, 1975; Watson 1987; Burrow 1981, pp. 221–22, 224–25). The relationship of these three hillforts is enigmatic. There is insufficient evidence to show whether they were all occupied over precisely the same period. Their sites were clearly chosen for their defensive potential, but their close proximity makes it difficult to perceive them as rival communities. If they were all occupied contemporaneously, some special role in a strategy aimed at controlling traffic through the Avon Gorge might be indicated. Some 10.5 km to the west, just beyond the point where the broad plateau narrows to a single ridge, is Cadbury Camp in Tickenham, a bivallate hillfort covering some 2.5 hectares (Grover 1875; Gray 1922; Burrow 1981, pp. 227–28). The last major site along the ridge, 6.5 km west of Cadbury, is a univallate promontory fort of 2.2 hectares on the coast at Wains Hill, Clevedon (Burrow 1981, p. 231).

Other nearby hillforts which need to be taken into account in calculating the potential territory available to those on the Failand ridge include Cadbury Camp at Congresbury, 7.5 km to the south (Fowler et al. 1970; Burrow 1981, pp. 217–18; Rahtz et al. 1992), and possibly also East Wood Hill at Portishead, at the northernmost tip of the coastal ridge, although the heavily disturbed nature of the earthworks here has brought its identification into question (Burrow 1924, p. 64; ApSimon 1957)

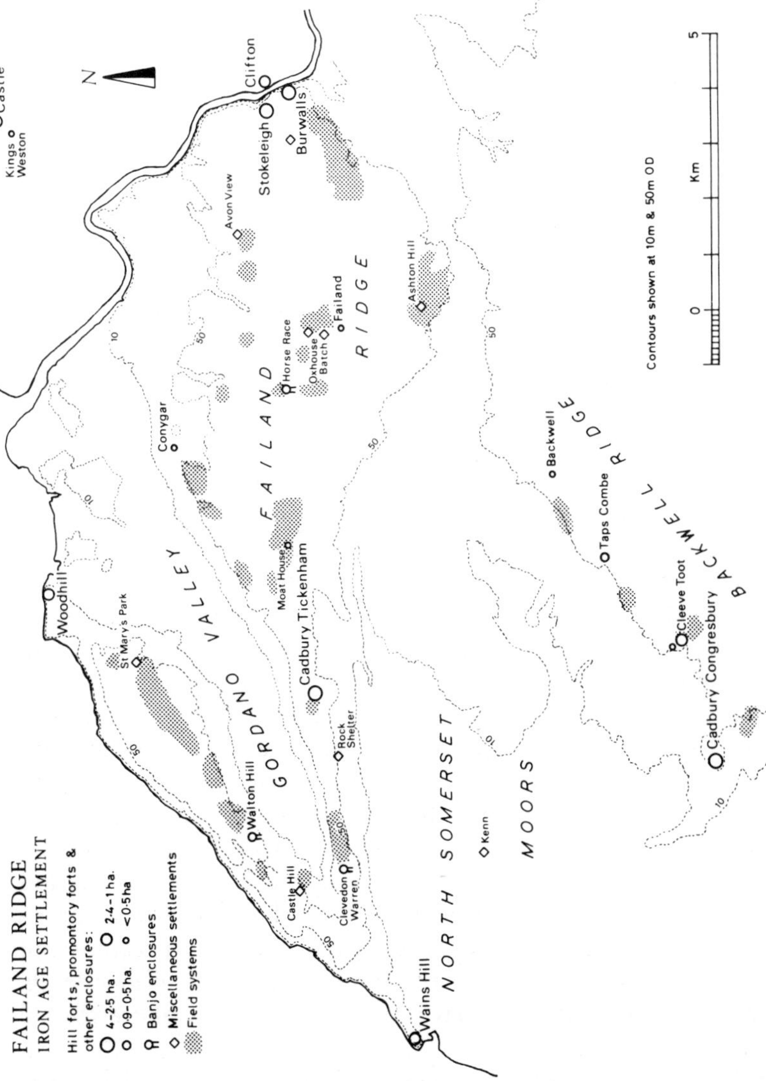

Fig. 6.1 Failand ridge. Iron Age settlement.

The major hillforts have, understandably, attracted a disproportionate amount of attention in the past, simply because they are so impressive. However, the Failand ridge, in common with the coastal ridge and the Backwell-Congresbury upland, also contains a considerable number of apparently contemporary smaller enclosures, including some of the distinctive 'banjo' type. Most of these have been catalogued and discussed by Gardner (1977). Excavation on several of these sites has revealed occupation continuing from the late prehistoric into the Roman period (Phillips 1931, 1933; Gardner 1977, pp. 163–66). Other occupation sites include a small cave about 1 km south-west of Cadbury Camp, which has produced some Iron Age pottery (Savory 1924).

What can be said of later prehistoric land use? The snail remains from the Court Hill barrow suggest that when the cairn was first constructed the local environment was a shaded one, with woodland and scrub near by, but the scatter of Iron Age and Romano-British pottery pointed to subsequent clearance and cultivation (Green 1973). Cereal cultivation was clearly a significant part of the economy at Cadbury Tickenham, as evidenced by two querns from the site, though the presence of pig bones and ash and oak charcoal point to the continuing survival of some woodland near by (Gray 1922, p. 13; Counc Br Archaeol Group 12/13 *Archaeol Rev* 2, 1967, p. 27). Several of the smaller prehistoric settlements along the ridge are still surrounded by traces of pre-medieval field systems, some irregular and curvilinear, some more rectilinear (Fowler 1978). Their precise dating is difficult, but their variety of form suggests a variety of origins and, perhaps, functions. Whatever their origin, many of them probably remained under cultivation throughout the Roman occupation. It is likely that those early field systems of which traces survive were always marginal, even when they occur in juxtaposition with known settlements. On the lower slopes, especially on the south, intensive medieval open field cultivation has obliterated all traces.

There is a fair amount of evidence for the use of the ridge during prehistory, but what of the moors on either side? Here the fundamental questions must be, at what period was the coastline stabilized in its present position and what was the nature and location of earlier coastlines? The northern Levels have not been subjected to palaeoenvironmental or archaeological investigations comparable with those carried out by the Somerset Levels Research Project south of the Mendip Hills. However, the proposals for the Severn Tidal Barrage and the Second Severn Crossing have recently prompted much new investigation of the estuary as a whole, and a complex picture of its alluvial stratigraphy is emerging (Rippon 1991, 1992, 1993). The post-glacial marine transgression appears to have reached its maximum around 2500–2200 BC. Through the later prehistoric period the area of the present moors is likely to have been partly intertidal, partly freshwater marsh. The laying of a new trunk sewer across Kenn Moor near Nailsea Wall in 1971 revealed a quantity of timber at some depth beneath the peat and estuarine silts which, it was suggested, might relate to a Neolithic or Bronze Age wooden platform or trackway linking the Kenn and Nailsea islands, similar to those discovered between the Mendip and Polden Hills (Gilbertson and Hawkins 1983); however, Coles (1984) has urged caution in making such deductions from the rather limited material salvaged. As yet there is no real evidence for any form of Iron Age occupation on the moors, though their use for wildfowling, fishing, and gathering reeds for thatching is likely, with summer grazing on the fringes.

It remains difficult to formulate any clear hypotheses about land division at this period. One attempt has been made to reconstruct theoretical territories attached to the local hillforts by means of Thiessen polygons (Burrow 1981, p. 25). On this basis, assuming that all the available land was attached to one hillfort or another, a territorial radius of between 3 km and 7 km can be deduced. Such an approach has some validity in highlighting the range of soil types and potential forms of land use available to each major settlement, but in such a topographically varied area it is of limited value in attempting to determine precise boundaries. Moreover, it fails to take account of variations in size and implied consequent variations in population and in territorial requirements. More sophisticated methods, such as the weighted Thiessen polygons used by Hogg (1971), or the XTENT model developed by Renfrew and Level (1979) and recommended by Grant (1986) have yet to be applied in this region.

In the meantime, can any headway be made with a more pragmatic approach, making the assumption of some degree of continuity and taking existing parish boundaries into consideration? It would be logical to suppose that the territory attached to the relatively isolated hillforts of Wains Hill and Cadbury Tickenham included land on both sides of the ridge, and that somewhere roughly midway between them lay a boundary in a north-south alignment. The western boundary of Tickenham parish follows a direct line from the moors to the crest of the ridge which would be nowhere more than 1 km off the line arrived at by the Thiessen polygon technique. However, much of this line follows a rhyne cut when the moors were drained in the nineteenth century, and in view of the likelihood that the moors were intercommoned in the Middle Ages it is difficult to make a convincing case for its antiquity. The present northern boundary of Tickenham also underwent minor modification in the nineteenth century, and although it now follows the line of the ridgeway track which itself has every appearance of considerable age, the fact that it passes so close to Cadbury must surely negate it as an Iron Age territorial boundary. If the dubious hillfort at Portishead has to be taken into the equation, then the northern boundary of Cadbury's territory would logically pass along the central axis of the Gordano valley; but here, too, the modern boundary separating Clapton from Weston and Portishead follows a nineteenth-century rhyne, and an earlier pattern of intercommoning seems likely. To the south the next major hillfort is Cadbury Congresbury; the River Kenn, which forms the southern limit of Nailsea, would provide a possible natural boundary. To the east, however, neither the natural topography nor the later parish bounds suggest any particularly obvious line, and the problem is compounded by the difficulty of deciding whether to treat Stokeleigh and Burwalls as one or two communities. Although some convincing claims have been made elsewhere for the continuity of prehistoric territorial boundaries through to later periods, here the question remains in doubt.

Romano–British Settlement

The imposition of Roman administration does not seem to have resulted in any immediate drastic change to the landscape of the Failand ridge. The majority of the rural population continued to live in farming settlements little different in their essential characteristics from their prehistoric predecessors, apart from the occasional replacement of wooden structures by stone buildings. Numerous rural settlements have been located through pottery concentrations, particularly along the southern side of the ridge, where in places they occur less than 1 km apart.

The most conspicuous new component of the Roman settlement pattern is a small group of villas, of which only one is on the Failand ridge itself (Fig. 6.2). Excavations at Gatcombe, near the southern foot of the ridge, have provided evidence for a small first-century AD farmstead, abandoned early in the third century. Later in the third century it was rebuilt on a much more elaborate scale, with massive stone defences enclosing at least 7 hectares (Branigan 1977). Other local villas appear modest by comparison. A villa on the Nailsea island just opposite Birdcombe Court in Wraxall parish was excavated in 1950–53, and produced evidence of occupation from *c.*250 to *c.*350 AD (Sykes 1951; Sykes and Brown 1961). The only known villa between the Failand ridge and the Channel coast lies on the outskirts of Portishead, where the Gordano valley opens to the sea: this has produced evidence for late third- and early fourth-century occupation, with signs of an earlier first-century phase abandoned due to flooding (Brown 1964–65).

Other villas may have existed which cannot now be authenticated. Two coin-hoards from Tickenham Hill and Clapton-in-Gordano were reported to have been found in association with extensive building foundations (Seyer 1821; Gardner 1977, 167–68). Collinson (1791 II, 304) refers to Roman coins, pottery and building foundations at Yanley in Long Ashton and at Portbury.

It is striking that none of the local villas can be recognized as such before the middle of the third century. It has been suggested that the whole area had been confiscated by the imperial authorities

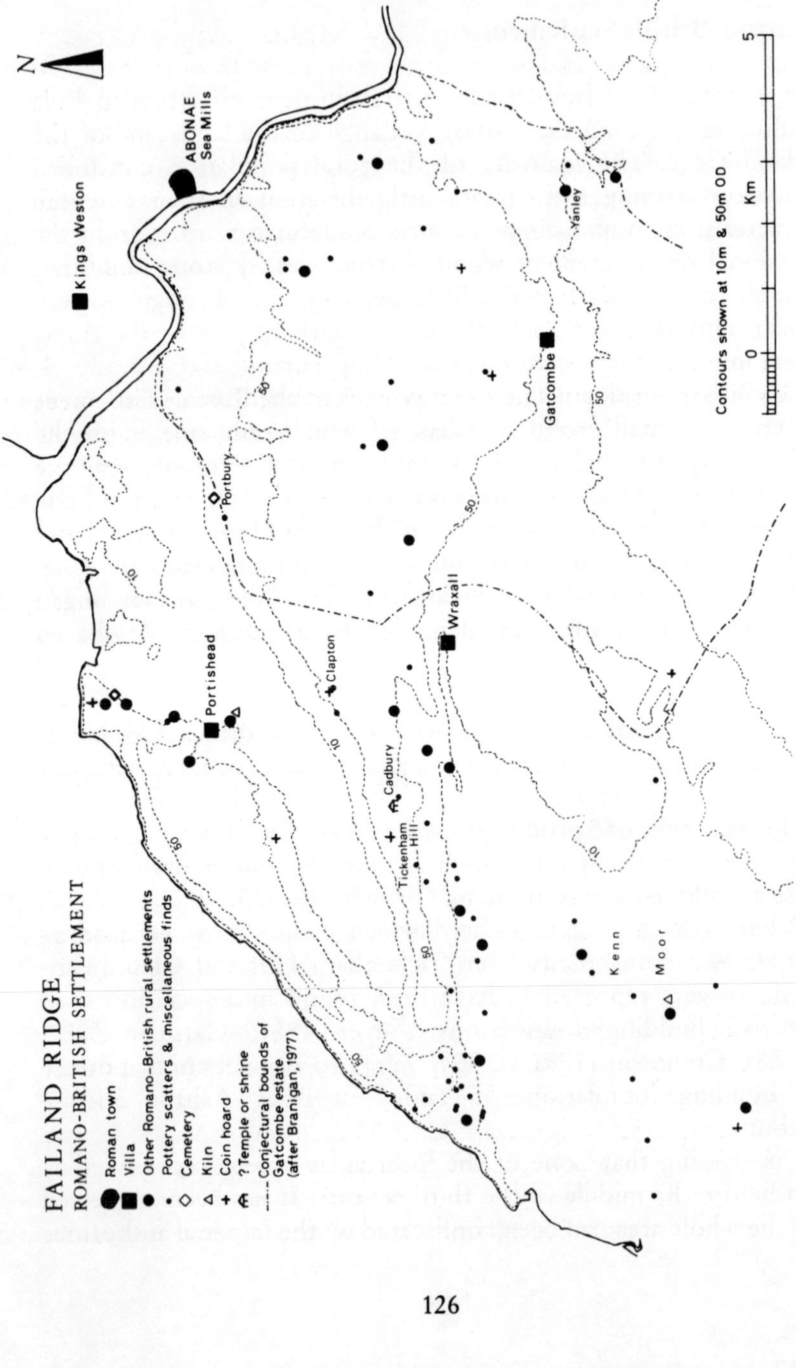

Fig. 6.2 Failand ridge. Romano-British settlement.

after the invasion in reprisal for local resistance, and that it was retained as an imperial estate until this period, when financial pressures finally prompted its dismemberment and sale. Villa owners fleeing from barbarian raids which had devastated the northern Gaulish frontier may have taken advantage of this opportunity for resettlement (Branigan 1973, 1976). The Wraxall villa included a space interpreted by Branigan as an intramural yard, a feature which he attributes to immigrant Gaulish landowners, though an alternative interpretation would see this as a large communal hall (Smith 1978).

The frontier of settlement was now extended out over the moors. During the 1960s a number of Romano-British sites were discovered on the alluvium down as far as the present line of the Middle Yeo, only a few metres above sea level. Further sites have been located on the low alluvial islands around Kenn (Lilly and Usher 1972). At Wemberham near Yatton there is evidence for a substantial villa right by the Congresbury Yeo, apparently occupied into the beginning of the fourth century (Scarth 1885; Reade 1885). Evidence for a similar advance onto the low land has been recorded beyond Mendip in the Brue and Axe valleys (McDonnell 1979). Some of these sites seem very vulnerable to flooding, given the high tidal range in the Bristol Channel, which hindered the outfall of the local streams. Further south the coast is naturally protected from marine inundation (though not from freshwater flooding) by sand dunes, but there is no evidence that the dune belt ever continued northwards beyond Middle Hope towards Clevedon. In order for settlement to be possible in these areas, some form of sea-wall must have existed in the Roman period, in addition to embankments along the major rivers (Rippon 1992). Indications of artificial drainage works of Romano-British date have come from one of the Kenn Moor sites (Lilly and Usher 1972). Little evidence has as yet been recovered from the inland peat moors of Congresbury, Nailsea, Tickenham or Clevedon, and these areas probably remained unreclaimed and unsettled, used only for fishing, wildfowling and perhaps summer pasture.

The agricultural landscape of the Roman period can be reconstructed in its broad outlines. Bone evidence from Gatcombe indicates large herds of cattle grazing the lower land. Cereal crops were grown, both on the plateau top and on the lower slopes; the evidence for corn milling and bakeries on the site suggests that production was on a commercial scale, producing a surplus for market as well as feeding the estate workforce. Vegetable gardens and orchards may have existed within the enclosure wall. Sheep were grazed, probably on the plateau top, for wool; pigs were also kept, largely for domestic consumption. Querns and a ploughshare have come from the site, though distinctive agricultural buildings such as barn, granary or livestock housing appear to be lacking within the walled complex itself (Branigan 1977). Several querns have also come from a site on Tickenham Hill in association with Roman pottery and coins (*Proc Somerset Archaeol & Nat Hist Soc* 27.i 1881, p. 76). One of the Kenn Moor sites included a corn-drying kiln, suggesting some intakes of arable land even on the alluvial flats (Lilly and Usher 1972).

Cunliffe (1966, pp. 71–72) has suggested that deteriorating conditions in the Levels in the late Roman period may have necessitated a change in the local economy away from farming towards industrial activities such as salt-working, pottery-making and metallurgical activities. One of the Kenn Moor sites has produced a considerable scatter of iron slag (Lilly and Usher 1972, p. 39). However, the general absence of briquetage or other industrial debris in the smaller rural settlements below the Failand ridge suggests that here the sea defences may have been effectively maintained and farming continued on all but the most intractable ground. Only at the Gatcombe villa, which is clearly a special case, is there evidence for iron, lead and pewter-working (Tylecote 1977).

During the early part of the Roman occupation the ridge top had ceased to be a favoured location for settlement. By the later third century this situation began to change. A Romano-British limestone relief, tentatively identified as an altar to Mars, was discovered in the inner ditch of Cadbury Tickenham hillfort in 1974 (Burrow and Bennett 1979). Pottery, tile and coins of Claudius Gothicus (AD 268–69) and Valentinian II (375–92) point to some form of reoccupation of the hillfort, perhaps in association with a temple or shrine (Gray 1922, p. 11; Burrow 1981, pp. 291–93). More substantial evidence of temples in comparable positions has come from Lydney, Cadbury Congresbury and Brean Down, possibly also Blaise Castle and Brent Knoll. This phenomenon may be linked with the evidence put forward by Branigan for an influx of settlers and capital from north-eastern Gaul at the very period when many of the local villas were being established (Branigan 1973; 1976, pp. 46–47). Perhaps because of the lack of major Roman towns nearby to serve as foci of Christian influence, pagan worship may have continued, or been reintroduced, long after the official adoption of Christianity (Burrow and Bennett 1979; Burrow 1981, pp. 161–62; Bird 1987).

Can anything be said of the pattern of Roman estates? It is difficult to find a basis for reconstructing the landed properties of the local villas. One problem is how to interpret the intervening 'native' settlements—were these independent communities farming their own land, or were they subsidiary settlements providing labour for the villa owners? Were the villas themselves in any way tenurially linked? Branigan has suggested that Gatcombe may have been the centre of a particularly large property containing several satellite villas, including Wraxall and Bedminster, each perhaps making some specialized contribution to the estate as a whole; its very unusual defences may, therefore, have provided a refuge for the occupants of these dependencies, as well as for Gatcombe itself (Branigan 1976, p. 90). Claims for the partial continuity of Roman estate boundaries into the Saxon period have been put forward in many areas, including the Vale of Wrington near by (Neale 1970), but it remains difficult to substantiate this on the Failand ridge. As Branigan has argued, exercises with Thiessen polygons on this matter are probably futile since Gatcombe appears to be in a different league from other local villas, and he proposes an outline for the Gatcombe estate comprising some 6,070 hectares based upon firm topographical limits which would leave sufficient land for its less wealthy neighbours, while still containing a variety of soils (Branigan 1977, pp. 192ff.). Very little of this proposed circuit can be made to coincide with later parish boundaries.

Post-Roman Settlement

The withdrawal of the Roman central administration appears to have been followed fairly rapidly by the breakdown of the commercial pottery industry and the cessation of coinage circulation, thereby removing two important classes of evidence from the archaeological record. There is no reason to suppose that this was accompanied by massive disruption or depopulation, however, and for the bulk of the population there was probably little immediate change in lifestyle. At Gatcombe there does appear to be a marked decline in material prosperity around AD 370–80, but some of the buildings were clearly reoccupied and remained in agricultural use into the fifth century, with a cemetery dating perhaps from the middle of the fifth century (Branigan 1977, pp. 178–79). At Wraxall there is some sign of squatter occupation at the close (Sykes 1951, p. 235). None of the local villas show any signs of violent destruction.

It was once thought that many parts of the Somerset Levels were again covered by the sea in the late or sub-Roman period, largely because Romano-British material found along the coastal clay belt was often sealed beneath up to 2 m of alluvial silt (Godwin 1943). Cunliffe's published plan (1966, p. 69), reconstructing the coastline at the period of supposed maximum marine transgression, shows the sea covering much of the Gordano valley and the coastal moors to a point well east of Kenn. However, subsequent research has suggested that the sea's incursion was less extensive than was formerly believed. Hawkins (1973) has argued that the present sea levels were attained no later than the Neolithic, and that in the Romano-British period the levels were in a transition stage between mud flats and grass saltings: the alluvium sealing Roman levels he believed to be a deposit recurringly laid down by high water spring tides. Such events are more likely to be a result of declining standards of sea-wall maintenance than of rising sea level. In the northern Levels in particular, Romano-British sites are often sealed by only about 0.15–0.6 m of estuarine clays, and this part of the lowland seems to have been relatively immune from the inundations which occurred elsewhere (Leech 1981; Rippon 1991, 1992).

Ian Burrow has presented the evidence for an extensive reuse of hillforts in the post-Roman period, suggesting a number of different motives: fear of attack from other groups within the region or from Saxons or Irish, the hillforts providing temporary refuges or permanent settlements or both; devolution of political control to local rulers who reoccupied sites of ancient power; religious beliefs involving a special veneration for hilltops; a social system requiring certain individuals to reside on hilltops as a mark of status; or a flight from environmental hazards such as flooding or disease on lower ground (Burrow 1981, pp. 149–71). Such reoccupation is best attested at Cadbury Congresbury (Rahtz et al. 1992). The limited scale of excavations on Cadbury Tickenham makes it difficult to guess whether this site was reused defensively in the post-Roman period, but if there was a late Roman pagan temple there, this may have survived as a cult centre for some time after the collapse of the imperial administration. There is also some evidence for the late Roman reoccupation of the Wains Hill fort at Clevedon (Burrow 1981, p. 294).

With the decline of urban life, the disappearance of the villa-owning aristocracy and the removal of the standing army, the countryside was under less pressure to produce agricultural surpluses, and there may have been a reversion to subsistence farming. This might be expected to lead to some abandonment of marginal land, in particular on the moors, where the land drains and sea walls probably fell into disrepair, and on the steeper slopes, where the area under woodland may have increased. The Old English place-names Long Ashton, *aesc-tūn*, 'enclosure or farmstead where ash-trees grow', and Abbot's Leigh, *lēah*, '?wood or woodland clearing', both may reflect the colonization of secondary woodland over abandoned farmland at the east end of the ridge (Ekwall 1960). However, the reoccupation of some hillforts may have led to a revival or even an extension of cultivation elsewhere on the ridge and plateau top.

The circumstances of the introduction of Christianity into the region remain a vexed question (Rahtz 1991). Cemeteries provide some evidence. At Portishead a group of forty-three east-west inhumations contained residual fourth-century material, while another early Christian cemetery was discovered during construction of Portbury school (Gardner 1977, p. 169). None of the local churches possess obvious minster characteristics: only Wraxall had dependent chapelries at Nailsea and Flax Bourton (Aston 1986, pp. 74–76).

It has often been suggested that the scatter of archaic church dedications to sixth-century 'Celtic' saints along the Somerset coast points to a survival of Roman or Celtic Christianity (Holmes 1911, pp. 1–4) or to early missions from Wales or Ireland (Porter 1971; Burrow 1981, p. 164; Rahtz 1982, p. 102). Examples in north Somerset include St Congar at Congresbury (now St Andrew), St Bridget at Chelvey and St Kew at Kewstoke (now St Paul). There is also a somewhat suspect tradition that Holy Trinity in Nailsea had an earlier dedication to St Padarn (Porter 1971, p. 23). Susan Pearce, however, has argued that there is little evidence for any traditions linking the commemorated saints with Somerset before the middle of the eleventh century, and suggests that many of these archaic dedications result from the deliberate promotion of Celtic saint cults by Glastonbury Abbey at a time when it was concerned to demonstrate its own antiquity (Pearce 1973, 1978, pp. 136–37). If the *Chiwestoch* of the Domesday survey is indeed Kewstoke rather than Chew Stoke (as argued by Morland 1954–55, p. 38), the association with St Kew goes back at least to the mid-eleventh century; if not, there is no record of the 'Kew' element before 1274. Chelvey's St Bridget dedication is not recorded until 1421, and this appears to be a name transferred from another estate of Sir Edmund de St Maur at Netherwent, west of Chepstow, where the church is similarly dedicated (Porter 1971, pp. 25–26). Only the St Congar association with Congresbury is secure, from Asser's description of the gift of the *monasterium* there in the 890s (Whitelock 1955, pp. 270–71).

Particular problems surround the dedication of Tickenham church to Saints Quiricus and Julietta, martyrs of the Diocletian persecution in Tarsus in AD 304. While this is not uncommon in France, Spain and Italy, only four other examples of the joint dedication are known in England, two in Cornwall, one in Devon and one in Cambridgeshire (Arnold-Forster 1899, I, 151–52,

170–72). Several speculative explanations for this exotic occurrence may be suggested:

(i) Was it a direct survival of Romano-British Christianity? Part of a third-century building has been recorded about 250 m east of the church, but there is no evidence that this was of any major significance. Nonetheless, evidence for Romano-British Christianity elsewhere on the ridge is provided by a sherd with a chi-rho graffito from a building at Gatcombe destroyed *c.*380 (Rahtz 1991, p.8).

(ii) Was it an early introduction from the Roman church on the continent? Auxerre, where some of the relics of Saints Quiricus and Julietta were enshrined, was a major centre of the cult, and it is a remote possibility that the dedication could have been introduced to Britain around the time of the visits of St Germanus of Auxerre in AD 429 and *c.*448.

(iii) Was it introduced in the fifth or sixth century from the Celtic church in Armorica, where the cult also appears to have had some popularity?

(iv) Was it brought to England after the Norman Conquest through the influence of French religious houses, as Arnold-Forster believed?

(v) Was it brought back from the homeland of the two martyrs in the eastern Mediterranean during or after the twelfth century by returning Crusaders or pilgrims?

Two points weaken the arguments for a post-Norman date. The concentration of the dedications in the south-west of Britain does not particularly favour the latter two options. Moreover, the decision taken by the Roman church in the sixth century to place the Acts of the two saints in a list of apocryphal documents to be rejected (Attwater 1965, p. 98) makes it questionable whether a new dedication would be countenanced by the mainstream church authorities, even if the cult remained popular in the world at large. On balance an introduction from Armorica seems most likely. Tickenham church itself contains no diagnostic pre-Conquest architecture; yet the considerable height of the nave and the very basic nature of the unmoulded narrow chancel arch with its simple imposts suggests an eleventh-century date.

Place-names containing Celtic elements occur to the south (Kenn, Kewstoke, Congresbury, Churchill), but along the Failand ridge and in the Gordano valley to the north the names are almost exclusively of Anglo-Saxon origin. The one possible exception, perhaps significantly, is Cadbury, where the first element may be the British word *catu* meaning battle or fortification (Hill 1914; Burrow 1981, pp. 51–52). Walton-in-Gordano, from its Domesday form *Waltone*, seems more likely to derive from Old English *w(e)ald-tūn*, 'farm in a wood', which would suit its location, rather than *w(e)ala-tūn*, 'farm of the Britons', but the latter cannot wholly be ruled out.

Of the Anglo-Saxon place-names, Long Ashton and Abbots Leigh have already been discussed. The second element of Portbury may imply some reuse of the small Conygar Hill earthwork (*burh*), while the first element may either be *port* in the sense of harbour (which presumes that one or both of the coastal inlets on the edge of the parish were navigable) or as a synonym for market. Although Portbury village today gives no impression of any special importance, it was formerly the centre of a hundred, which probably consisted originally of ten tithings, the six Gordano villages plus Clevedon, Tickenham, Nailsea and Wraxall (Wigan n.d. pp. 18–25). The locally prominent Conygar Hill was probably the original hundred meeting-place, though subsequently the hundred courts appear to have met in the manor-house. In 1348 Maurice de Berkeley acquired a charter for a market and two annual fairs at Portbury, which may have been an endorsement of a prescriptive market of much greater antiquity. Portbury remained the only place in the hundred with a market throughout the Middle Ages, though Clevedon, Weston-in-Gordano and Wraxall all possessed fairs (Hulbert 1936, pp. 104–5). The occurrence nearby of the topographical place-name Portishead, 'headland or ridge-end (*hēafod*) by the harbour', suggests that the first element is more likely here to mean 'harbour' than 'market'. Easton- and Weston-in-Gordano may be named in relation to Portbury, as the early 'central place', or with respect to their position in the Gordano valley.

Clapton incorporates the Old English *clop*, hillock or hill, a puzzling name since there is nothing especially distinctive about its location within the context of the Failand ridge as a whole. Clevedon is the topographical name *clif* (gen. pl. *clifa*) + *dun*, 'hill of the cliffs'. Tickenham may be 'Tica's *hām*', though it would be unwise to identify this individual with the so-named eighth-century Abbot of Glastonbury, in view of the lack of any known connection with the Abbey (*contra* Burrow 1981, p. 53); it may alternatively incorporate an earlier name for the Yeo, *æt-icken-hām*. Wraxall probably incorporates the element *halh*, meaning something like 'secluded valley', which could describe the coomb above the church, but the first element remains obscure (Ekwall 1960).[2]

Medieval and Post-medieval

The identification of territorial units becomes clearer in the Middle Ages with the emergence of the parish system. Unfortunately the lack of pre-Conquest charters with boundary clauses in this part of Somerset makes it difficult to establish the antiquity of these units, in particular their relationship to Anglo-Saxon and earlier estates.

What does emerge from an examination of parish boundaries is their lack of regularity (Fig. 6.3). They vary in size from the 1,527 hectares of Wraxall (excluding its chapelries of Nailsea and Flax Bourton, where the intricate intervening boundaries betray their former association) down to the 287 hectares of Weston-in-Gordano. They do not accord well with a network of Thiessen polygons based upon the ancient parish churches; nor do they display the characteristic strip-like pattern of the central Polden parishes, crossing the geological grain of the countryside; indeed, in so far as there is any observable relationship, the general orientation of the parishes tends to follow the geological strike

2 *Editor's note*: for Wraxall, Mills (ibid., p. 372) suggests Old English **wrocc* + *halh*, 'nook of land frequented by the buzzard or other bird of prey'.

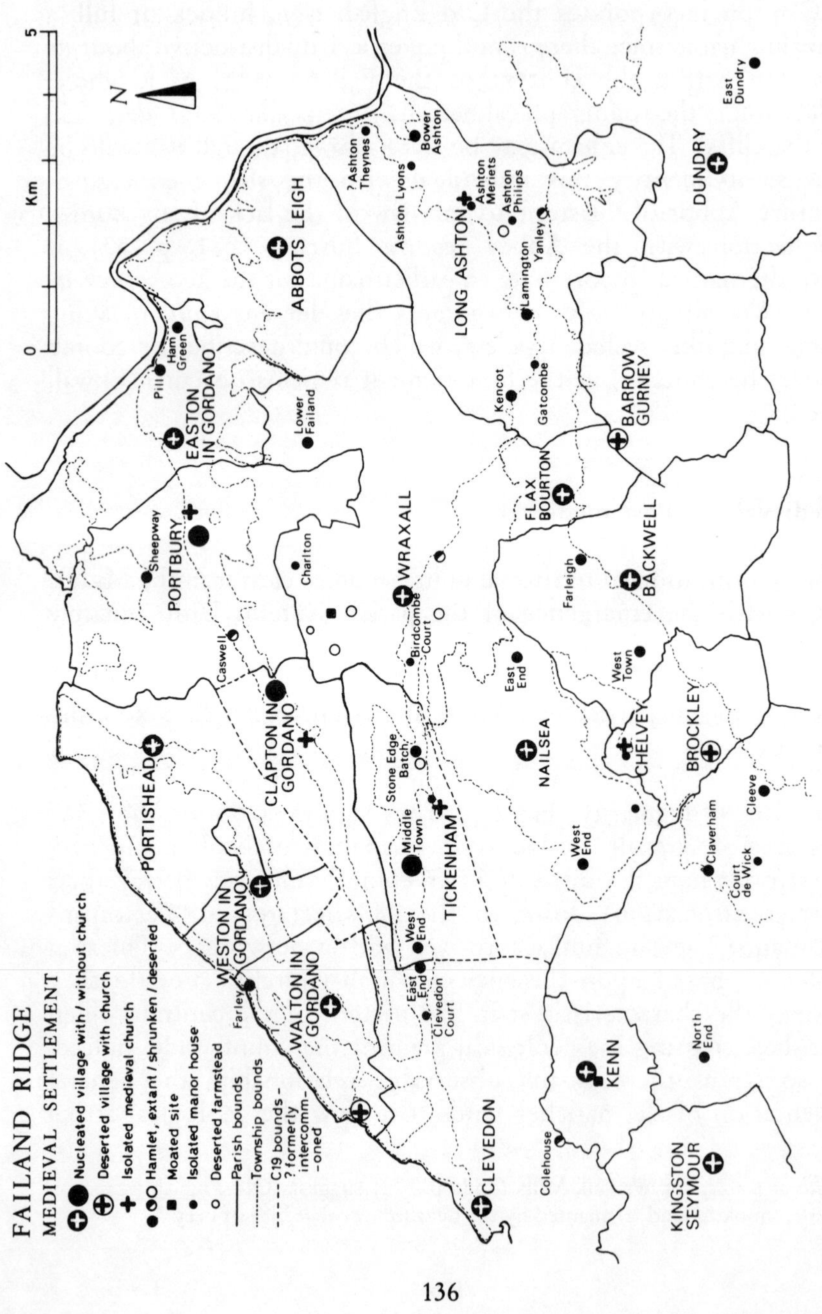

Fig. 6.3 Failand ridge. Medieval settlement.

rather than straddle it. Relatively few of the boundaries follow well-marked natural features: it is particularly striking that the watershed along the top of the ridge is utilized as a parish boundary only for about 5 km between Clapton-in-Gordano, Tickenham and a small part of Clevedon: the east end of the Tickenham boundary also follows the contour around the head of the Little Valley. Despite this, each parish does succeed in taking advantage of the variation of natural topography to maximize its range of land use options. All of the parishes with land on the ridge also include land on the lower slopes and all but the two most easterly parishes (Abbots Leigh and Long Ashton) include a substantial amount of land on the low moors. The origins of the parish boundaries require further examination, but on present evidence it is difficult to envisage the general arrangement existing before the early Middle Ages.

The four broad zones of land use previously identified can now be documented more fully:

(i) Many of the higher parts of the ridge, previously under arable cultivation, now went down to permanent pasture, thereby preserving traces of the earlier field systems as earthworks. Some of these grasslands were used as commons into the nineteenth century. Later in the Middle Ages some parts were used as manorial rabbit-warrens: pillow-mounds survive on Wains Hill and Dial Hill at Clevedon, and warrens are documented or implied by place-names at Clevedon (Conygar), Portbury (Conygar Hill) and Failand Lodge Farm (The Warren).

(ii) The steep slopes on either side for the most part remained wooded. Most of the woodland attributed to the vills along the ridge in the Domesday survey probably lay on these slopes, rather than at a greater distance. While no satisfactory general formula for translating Domesday woodland dimensions into meaningful acreages has ever been devised, nonetheless local examination sometimes suggests solutions. Taking one example at random, Tickenham's woodland in 1086 consisted of 110 acres on the principal manor of William de Eu, and it is conspicuous that the combined extent of Lime Breach Wood and Chummock Wood, the largest contiguous block of woodland in the parish, was just over

113 acres (*c.*46 hectares) in the 1840s.[3] There was an additional 3 × 1 furlongs on a smaller estate and these dimensions are not very different from those of Bays Wood, the nearest woodland to Barrow Court, the centre of this smaller manor. There is an argument here, not only for the antiquity of much of the existing woodland within the parish, but also for some stability in its shape and extent.

The botanical constituents of woodlands sometimes underline their antiquity. Small-leaved lime (*Tilia cordata*), which is sensitive to grazing and slow to colonize new sites, was probably the dominant tree of the primeval forest in this part of Britain, and since it has rarely been deliberately planted for commercial purposes, its presence is likely to indicate woodland of considerable age, perhaps in a few cases woodland which has never been cleared. Tickenham's Lime Breach Wood contains much small-leaved lime, together with oak, ash, hornbeam, hazel, whitebeam, wild service and gean. Wayfaring tree and spindle occur on the margins. Its ground flora includes bluebell, wood anemone, dogs mercury, spurge laurel, fly orchis and twayblade orchid. There is a wide range of mosses and lichens. At the east end of the Failand ridge, the northern part of Leigh Woods in Abbots Leigh, dropping down to the Avon Gorge, is old coppicewood dominated by small-leaved lime, with ash, oak hazel and occasional wild service, and a ground flora including lily-of-the-valley. This part of the wood, which belonged to the canons of St Augustine's in Bristol, is documented back to the early fourteenth century, and was managed by coppicing throughout the Middle Ages (Rackham 1982). It seems possible that some of these woods have never been cleared, and are directly descended from the prehistoric woodland. However, since the Middle Ages they have been greatly modified. Exotic introductions such as Monterey pine and larch have appeared in Lime Breach Wood, while sycamore invasion is a problem in Leigh Woods and elsewhere.

Some indications of local medieval clearance can be deduced from the evidence of irregular field shapes, hedges containing

[3]Somerset County Record Office D/D/Rt 433.

woodland relict species and field-names incorporating words such as the Middle English *breche*, meaning 'land newly taken into cultivation'. In Tickenham the tithe map shows two fields called 'Breach' at the head of the Little Valley below Chummock Wood, and another with a very irregular outline bitten into the south-western angle of Lime Breach Wood,[4] but there is little evidence that agricultural encroachments made any extensive inroads into the woodlands.

Elsewhere it is clear that the woodland margins have expanded. The southern part of Leigh Woods in Long Ashton parish encroaches over the earthworks of Stokeleigh Camp, and Rackham (1982) has shown that this part is different in character from the more ancient northern part, containing many old pollard oaks of 200–400 years, with occasional limes, and maiden ash and wych-elm no more than 150 years old. Through the Middle Ages this area was a wood-pasture common, where the trees belonged to the landowner but the grassland remained available for common grazing, an arrangement first documented in 1331–33. The elimination of grazing rights in the mid-nineteenth century allowed the expansion of secondary woodland dominated by ash and wych-elm over the old pasture.

Several manorial deer parks were enclosed during the Middle Ages, with locations chosen on the wooded slopes of the narrower part of the ridge, or in the more broken country of the broader plateau to the east, where the land was generally less attractive for cultivation. At both Clevedon and Wraxall the parks are first recorded in 1322 in a complaint of illicit hunting and theft of deer made by their respective owners (*Cal Pat Rolls, 1321–24*, p. 252). Long Ashton Park was first created by an emparking licence granted to Thomas Lyons in 1393 (*Cal Charter Rolls V, 1341–1417*, p. 334). All the medieval parks have been altered in size and landscaped at later periods, a process which cannot be followed here.

(iii) The gentler slopes below the woodland, down to the moors on either side, were covered by cultivated fields. During the Middle

[4]Ibid.

Ages much of this was under open field cultivation. As yet it remains unclear when this form of cultivation first took shape in this particular area, and there is very little direct evidence for the number of fields in any given parish, or their precise extent. Further investigation of the nature of local open field cultivation should be a prime target of future research.

Limited early enclosures may be implied by field-names such as Tynings (Old English *tȳning*, 'enclosure'), Gastons (Old English *gærstūn*, 'grass enclosure or paddock') and New Crofts, all occurring in Tickenham. Most of the open field land was enclosed after the end of the Middle Ages, but relatively little survived sufficiently late to be dealt with under the parliamentary procedure. In Tickenham the tithe map suggests more than one period of enclosure. In the western part of the parish the field pattern is strongly linear, some of the bounds with distinct aratral curves, suggesting a process of consolidation and enclosure by agreement from open field, perhaps in the sixteenth or seventeenth century. Eastwards from the church the fields are generally of more rectangular shape, but the occurrence of 'acre' and 'lands' names suggests that this area too was once under open field cultivation.[5] An unspecified area of open field in the North Field and Great North Field of Wraxall was dealt with under an enclosure award of 1819, and some common arable and meadow survived in Long Ashton until 1820 (Tate 1948). As with the extent of open fields, much more work is needed on the local history of pre-parliamentary enclosure.

(iv) Large parts of the moors continued to provide fishing, wildfowling and summer grazing, and some parts may well have been intercommoned. Part of Tickenham Moor was used as a turbary: St Mark's Hospital in Bristol acquired the right to dig turf there from Nicholas, son of Roger FitzNicholas, then lord of Tickenham (d.1261) (Collinson, 1791, III, 164). More advanced forms of some of the traditional usages are represented, for example, by the duck decoys at North Weston and Walton in the Gordano valley and on Kenn Moor (McDonnell 1984).

[5]Ibid.

The reclamation of parts of the estuarine clay belt may have commenced in the eighth or ninth century (Rippon 1993). The pattern of very irregular field boundaries and sinuous droves and rhynes immediately south of Clevedon, continuing through the parishes of Kingston Seymour and Wick St Lawrence, seems to be of early medieval origin, contrasting sharply with the very rectilinear layouts on the peat moors further inland, where drainage and enclosure was delayed until the beginning of the nineteenth century. Even then, frequent and prolonged flooding remained a problem, not finally solved until 1949–53, when the sea walls were reinforced and a new outfall channel, the Blind Yeo, was cut through to the sea at Clevedon (Tate 1948; Williams 1964; 1970, pp. 242–43).

While the basic pattern of land use remained relatively stable through the Middle Ages and beyond, the pattern of settlement appears remarkably fluid, with the development of nucleated villages beginning late and being imperfectly achieved. In Tickenham the church stands virtually isolated on the edge of the moor, at the end of a long spur coming down from the main ridge (Fig. 6.4). Until recently only the fifteenth-century Tickenham Court with its outbuildings stood near by (Forrest 1975). The last knoll on the spur, west of the Court, is encircled by slight earthworks which hint at an earlier manorial site; however, there is little evidence of, or room for, any larger nucleated settlement here. The present main village, Middle Town, and the hamlet of West End, both seem to have settled on top of what had previously been open field land. The remaining hamlet in the parish, Stone Edge Batch, is a group of three farms and several cottages originally arranged around a small rectangular green. Earthworks below Stone Edge Batch towards the church suggest a former area of settlement, and recent evaluation trenches in advance of gas pipeline construction produced some structural evidence and pottery from the thirteenth century into the post-medieval period (Newns 1993; Parry 1993); but the circumstances under which this was abandoned and the period when present hamlets took shape remains unknown. At Wraxall there are two main settlement nuclei, one around the church, one 0.5 km to the south-east, with the earthworks of a third settlement

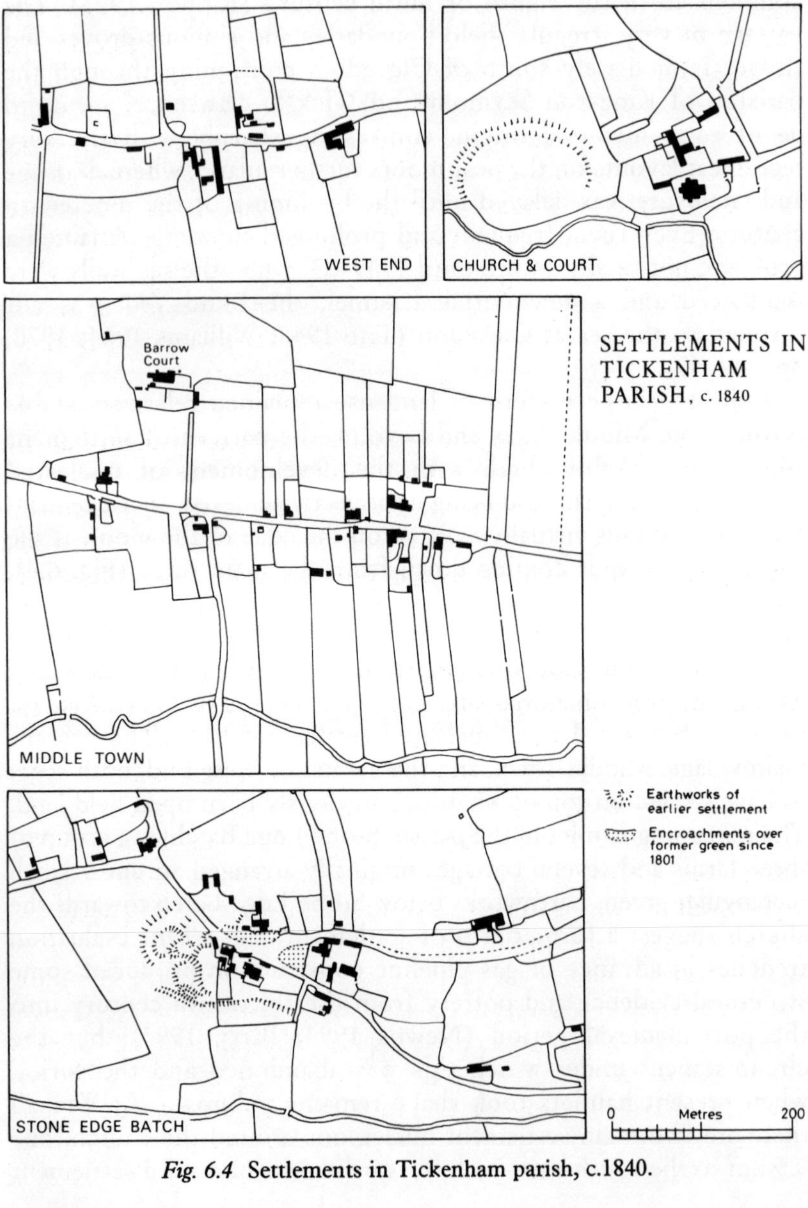

Fig. 6.4 Settlements in Tickenham parish, c.1840.

just above flood level near the valley bottom. In addition, in the west of the parish the ruins of the Roman villa seem to have survived sufficiently intact to be reoccupied in the thirteenth and fourteenth centuries (Sykes 1951), then being levelled and perhaps succeeded by Birdcombe Court, which incorporates the remains of a fourteenth-century hall and fifteenth-century cross-wing (Bismanis 1977; Williams and Gilson 1981). Moat House Farm in the north may similarly be the successor to an abandoned thirteenth-century longhouse near by (Gardner 1977, p. 164). Long Ashton and Abbots Leigh both today have a strongly linear plan, but Long Ashton also has several other settlement nuclei at Bower Ashton, Yanley and Gatcombe. In addition, earthworks north of Lower Court Farm, itself a house partly of fifteenth-century origin, have been identified as a possible deserted hamlet on the manor of Ashton Philips. Three of the eleven possible tofts identified by survey provided evidence of use from the eleventh to thirteenth centuries; however, while the excavation recovered a considerable quantity of pottery, there was little structural evidence or other settlement debris, and it remains possible that these enclosures were gardens or paddocks associated with a succession of mills (Leech and Pearson 1986).

A similar degree of settlement mobility during and since the Middle Ages can be demonstrated on the coastal ridge and on the Nailsea island. The present village of Walton-in-Gordano lies on the eastern side of the coastal ridge, overlooking the Gordano moors. However, its medieval church, ruined and isolated by the eighteenth century, stood on the coast 1.5 km to the west. Any settlement near the old church may have been eliminated by eighteenth-century emparkment; however, the present village site may itself have been occupied by the thirteenth century, since four of the twenty-two contributors to the 1327 Lay Subsidy at Walton bear the name 'Bythemor'. A new church was built in the present village in 1839, while the old church was rebuilt in 1870 to serve the growing villa suburbs of Clevedon. At Nailsea, Margaret Thomas has shown how the medieval agricultural nucleus around Holy Trinity church was overtaken by the development of Kingshill, 0.7 km to the north-west, following the discovery of coal there in

Profile of Failand Ridge: Changes in Land Use

	Zone 1a coastal clay belt & alluvial islands	Zone 1b Peat moors	Zone 2 Lower slopes	Zone 3 Steeper slopes	Zone 4 Ridge / plateau top
Iron Age	Seasonal flooding		?Enclosed arable	Woodland	Enclosed arable & upland pasture
	Summer pasture	Fishing Wildfowling Reeds			
Romano-British	Sea defences		Enclosed arable	?Reduced woodland extent	Enclosed arable & upland sheep pasture
	Small arable intakes Drained pasture Haymeadows	Fishing Wildfowling			
Post-Roman	Breakdown of seasonal defences Seasonal flooding Abandonment of marginal arable		?Reduced enclosed arable	?Increased woodland extent	?Limited increase in arable land
Late Medieval	Enclosed pasture & meadow	Common pasture Fishing Wildfowling Turbary	Open-field arable	Woodland Deer parks	Enclosed & common pasture Rabbit warrens
Post-Medieval C16-17	Enclosed pasture & meadow	Common pasture	Open-field arable, locally enclosed by agreement	Woodland	Enclosed & common pasture Rabbit warrens
Post-Medieval C18-20	Enclosed pasture & meadow	Parliamentary enclosure Drained & enclosed pasture	Enclosed arable & pasture Market gardens	Woodland Landscape parks	Parliamentary enclosure Enclosed pasture

Fig. 6.5 Profile of Failand ridge: (a) changes in land use.

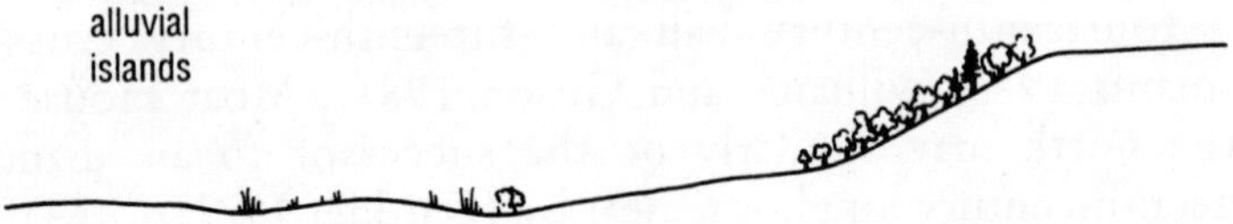

Profile of Failand Ridge: Changes in Settlement Pattern

		Zone 1a coastal clay belt & alluvial islands	Zone 1b Peat moors	Zone 2 Lower slopes	Zone 3 Steeper slopes	Zone 4 Ridge / plateau top
Iron Age						Hill forts Banjo enclosures Enclosed & unenclosed farmsteads
Romano- British		Small no. of villas & unenclosed farmsteads		Villas & unenclosed farmsteads		Abandonment of hill forts Continued occupation of some farmsteads
Post- Roman		Abandonment of settlements		Squatter reoccupation of some villas		Reoccupation of some hillforts ?Pagan temples
Late Medieval		Hamlets Isolated farmsteads		New nucleated villages Hamlets Isolated farmsteads Manor houses Churches		Hamlets Isolated farmsteads
Post-Medieval	C16-17	Hamlets Isolated farmsteads		Localised village contraction & desertion	Large country houses	Hamlets Isolated farmsteads
	C18-20	Hamlets Isolated farmsteads		New estate villages New enclosure farms Suburbanisation of existing villages		Squatting encroach- ments on commons New suburban villages

Fig. 6.5 Profile of Failand ridge: (b) changes in settlement pattern

the fifteenth century; then, as the glassworks developed as a major employer in the nineteenth century, the focus of settlement moved eastwards, initially to the old enclosures around the margins of Nailsea Heath, then along the new High Street following the heath's enclosure in 1813–19. Out beyond these central areas were two irregular dispersed settlements of agricultural character, West End and East End (Thomas 1984).

Conclusion

The traditional picture of a major disruption at the end of the Roman period, followed by a radical change under the Anglo-Saxons, when pioneer settlers were envisaged as colonizing a sparsely-inhabited wilderness with new forms of nucleated village and communally-worked field systems, which then remained relatively stable into the early modern period, has long been untenable. Much of the thrust of research over the past few decades has been aimed towards demonstrating aspects of continuity from the Romano-British or prehistoric periods. The early Anglo-Saxon period can no longer be seen as the great formative period in the history of the landscape. However, the debate about continuity continues to be bedevilled by confusion resulting from the indiscriminate use of the term: are we talking about long-term unbroken habitation on the same piece of ground; continuity of community, with succeeding generations living within the same general area; continuity of political control; continuity of agrarian regime; unbroken descent of estate ownership or tenurial arrangements; or continuity of estate boundaries?

So far as the Failand ridge is concerned, the evidence is mixed. Current impressions indicate a considerable element of continuity of land use, at least in terms of woodland and open country, though the precise extent, location and boundaries of arable, grassland and woodland have varied (Fig 6.5a). There is perhaps also an assumption of genetic continuity rather than population replacement; but by the seventh century the imposition of West Saxon political control, the adoption of the English language and the spread of

Christianity had created a new cultural environment. At present there seems little evidence for tenurial continuity or the persistence of estate boundaries. Even less can be said in favour of continuity of settlement location; indeed, considerable mobility is indicated, and settlements seem to be the least stable elements of this landscape at all periods (Fig 6.5b). This need not surprise us: chronological variations in the location and form of settlement reflect the changing nature of society and the changing requirements and aspirations of individuals and groups within it. However, much more work is required before these changes can fully be understood.

Acknowledgements

Most of the content of this essay has depended upon the work of others, whose contributions are listed in the references below. I am grateful to Rob Iles, former County Archaeologist for Avon, for supplying me with details on Tickenham from the Avon Sites and Monuments Record some years ago. I would also like to thank Vince Russett, the present County Archaeologist, and David Evans, SMR Officer, for their most helpful and efficient response to my request for an update on recent work and further information on other parishes despite the ridiculously short notice I gave them. Finally I would like to thank Della Hooke for inviting me to contribute to this volume and for forcing me to concentrate my mind upon the problems outlined above.

References

Anderson, C.F., Dagnall, J.M.M. and Marriott, E.M., 1989. 'A crouched inhumation at Tickenham, Avon', *Bristol & Avon Archaeology*, 8, pp. 48–50.

Arnold-Forster, F., 1899. *Studies in Church Dedications*, 3 vols (London).

ApSimon, A., 1957. 'East Wood, Portishead', *Proc Univ Bristol Spelaeol Soc*, 8. i, p. 40.

Aston, M., 1986. 'Post-Roman central places in Somerset', in *Central Places, Archaeology and History*, ed. E. Grant (Sheffield), pp. 74–6.

Atkinson, G.M., 1868–69. 'Clifton Camps', *Proc Somerset Archaeol & Nat Hist Soc*, 15. ii, pp. 27–31.

Attwater, D., 1965. *The Penguin Dictionary of Saints* (Harmondsworth).

Bird, S., 1987. 'Roman Avon', in *The Archaeology of Avon: a Review from the Neolithic to the Middle Ages*, ed. M. Aston and R. Iles (Avon City Council, Bristol), pp. 52–71.

Bismanis, M.R., 1977. 'Birdcombe Court, Wraxall, Avon: a fifteenth-century house', *Archaeological Journal*, 134, pp. 303–6.

Branigan, K., 1973. 'Gauls in Gloucestershire?' *Trans Bristol & Gloucestershire Archaeol Soc*, 92, pp. 82–95.

Branigan, K., 1976. *The Roman Villa in South-West England* (Bradford-on-Avon).

Branigan, K., 1977. *Gatcombe: the Excavation and Study of a Romano-British Villa Estate, 1967–1976*, Br Archaeol Rep, Br ser, 44 (Oxford).

Brown, J.C., 1964–65. 'A Romano-British site at St Mary's Lane, Portishead, Somerset', *Proc Univ Bristol Spelaeol Soc*, 10. iii, pp. 259–71.

Burrow, I., 1981. *Hillfort and Hill-top Settlement in Somerset in the First to Eighth Centuries AD*, Br Archaeol Rep, Br Ser, 91 (Oxford).

Burrow, I. and Bennett, J., 1979. 'A Romano-British relief from Cadbury Camp, Tickenham, Avon', in *Rescue Archaeology in the Bristol Area, 1*, ed. N. Thomas, City of Bristol Museum & Art Gallery Monograph 2, pp. 1–4.

Chisholm, M., 1962. *Rural Settlement and Land Use* (London).

Coles, J.M., 1984. 'One swallow, one summer? a comment on a wooden stake in Kenn Moor', *Proc Somerset Archaeol & Nat Hist Soc*, 128, p. 31.

Collinson, J., 1791. *The History and Antiquities of the County of Somerset*, 3 vols (Bath).

Cunliffe, B., 1966. 'The Somerset Levels in the Roman period', in *Rural Settlement in Roman Britain*, ed. C. Thomas, Counc Br Archaeol Res Rep, 7 (London) pp. 68–73.

Darvill, 1987. 'Neolithic Avon: 3500–1650 b.c.', in *The Archaeology of Avon*, ed. M. Aston and R. Iles, pp. 12–27.

Dawkins, W. Boyd, 1906. 'Early man', in *VCH Somerset*, 1 (London), pp. 167–204.

Dobson, D.P., 1931. *The Archaeology of Somerset* (London).

Ekwall, E., 1960. *The Concise Oxford Dictionary of English Place-Names*, 4th edn. (Oxford).

Faull, M.L. (ed.) 1984. *Studies in Late Anglo-Saxon Settlement* (Oxford Univ Dep External Stud).

Forrest, D., 1975. *The Making of a Manor: the Story of Tickenham Court* (Bradford-on-Avon).

Fowler, P.J., 1978. 'Pre-medieval fields in the Bristol region', in *Early Land Allotment in the British Isles: a Survey of Recent Work*, ed. H.C. Bowen and P.J. Fowler, Br Archaeol Rep, Br Ser, 48 (Oxford), pp. 29–47.

Fowler, P.J., Gardner, K.S. and Rahtz, P.A., 1970. *Cadbury Congresbury, Somerset, 1968* (Bristol).

Gardner, K., 1977. 'The Gatcombe area in the Roman period', in *Gatcombe*, ed. K. Branigan (Oxford), pp. 161–74.

Gilbertson, D.D. and Hawkins, A.B., 1983. 'A prehistoric wooden stake and the alluvial stratigraphy of Kenn Moor, Avon', *Proc Somerset Archaeol & Nat Hist Soc* 127, pp. 1–6.

Godwin, H., 1943. 'Coastal peat beds of the British Isles and North Sea', *Journal of Ecology*, 31, pp. 199–246.

Grant, E., 1986. 'Hill forts central places and territories', in *Central Places, Archaeology and History*, ed. E. Grant (Sheffield) pp. 13–26.

Gray, H. St. G., 1922. 'Trial excavations at Cadbury Camp, Tickenham, Somerset', *Proc Somerset Archaeol & Nat Hist Soc*, 68. ii, pp. 8–20.

Green, H.S., 1973. 'Archaeology and the M5 motorway, 5th report: the excavation of a round cairn on Court Hill, Tickenham, North Somerset, 1969', *Proc Somerset Archaeol & Nat Hist Soc*, 117, pp. 33–44.

Grinsell, L.V., 1971. 'Somerset barrows; part II: north and east', *Proc Somerset Archaeol & Nat Hist Soc*, 115 Suppl, pp. 43–137.

Grover, J.W., 1875. 'Cadbury Camp and similar works near Bristol', *J Br Archaeol Assoc*, 31, pp. 68–75.

Haldane, J.W., 1965–6. 'Stokeleigh Camp, Somerset', *Proc Univ Bristol Spelaeol Soc*, 11. i, pp. 31–8.

Haldane, J.W., 1975. 'Excavations at Stokeleigh Camp, Avon', *Proc Univ Bristol Spelaeol Soc*, 14. i, pp. 29–63.

Hawkins, A.B. 1973. 'Sea-level changes around south-west England', in *Marine Archaeology*, ed. D. Blackman, Colston Papers (Bristol), pp. 66–87.

Hill, J.S., 1914. *The Place Names of Somerset* (Bristol).

Hogg, A.H.A., 1971. 'Some applications of surface fieldwork', in *The Iron Age and its Hill Forts*, ed. D. Hill and M. Jesson (Southampton), pp. 105–25.

Holmes, T. Scott, 1911. 'Ecclesiastical history', in *VCH Somerset*, 2, pp. 1–4.

Hooke, D. (ed.), 1988. *Anglo-Saxon Settlements* (Oxford).

Hulbert, N.F., 1936. 'A survey of the Somerset fairs', *Proc Somerset Archaeol & Nat Hist Soc*, 82, pp. 104–5.

Leech, R.H., 1981. 'The Somerset Levels in the Romano-British period', in *The Evolution of Marshland Landscapes*, ed R.T. Rowley, (Oxford University Dep. External Stud.) pp. 20–51.

Leech, R.H. and Pearson, T., 1986. 'Excavations at Lower Court Farm, Long Ashton', *Bristol & Avon Archeology*, 5, pp. 12–35.

Lilly, D. and Usher, G., 1972. 'Romano-British sites on the North Somerset Levels', *Proc Univ Bristol Spelaeol Soc*, 13. i, pp. 37–40.

McDonnell, R., 1979. 'The Upper Axe Valley: an interim statement', *Proc Somerset Archaeol & Nat Hist Soc*, 123, pp. 75–82.

McDonnell, R.R.S., 1984. 'Duck decoys in Somerset: a gazetteer', *Proc Somerset Archaeol & Nat Hist Soc*, 128, pp. 25–30.

Morgan, C. Lloyd, 1900. 'Notes on Clifton, Burwalls and Stokeleigh Camps', *Clifton Antiquarian Club*, 5, pp. 8–24.

Morgan, C. Lloyd, 1901. 'Burwalls and Stokeleigh Camps', *Proc Somerset Archaeol & Nat Hist Soc*, 47. ii, pp. 217–29.

Morland, S.C., 1954–5. 'Some Domesday manors', *Proc Somerset Archaeol & Nat Hist Soc*, 99/100, pp. 38–48.

Neale, F., 1970. 'Early history', in 'Fieldwork and excavation in the Butcombe area, North Somerset', ed. P.J. Fowler, *Proc Univ Bristol Spelaeol Soc*, 12. ii, pp. 171–75.

Newns, S.C., 1993. *Portbury to Nailsea Gas Pipeline, British Gas PLC (South Western): a Preliminary Assessment of the Archaeological Implications* (Avon Archaeological Unit).

Parry, A.H.H., 1993. *An Archaeological Investigation of Sites within the Construction Corridor of the Portbury to Nailsea Gas Pipeline on behalf of British Gas PLC* (South Western) (Avon Archaeological Unit).

Pearce, S.M., 1973. 'The dating of some Celtic dedications and the hagiographical traditions of south-western Britain', *Rep & Trans Devonshire Assoc*, 105, pp. 95–120.

Pearce, S.M., 1978. *The Kingdom of Dumnonia: Studies in History and Tradition in South-Western Britain, AD 350–1150* (Padstow).

Phillips, C.W., 1931. 'Earthworks on Walton Common Down, near Clevedon', *Proc Univ Bristol Spelaeol Soc*, 4. i, pp. 34–42.

Phillips, C.W., 1933, 'Note on excavations at Wraxall', *Proc Univ Bristol Spelaeol Soc*, 4. ii, p. 150.

Porter, H.M., 1971. *The Celtic Church in Somerset* (Bath).

Rackham, O., 1982. 'The Avon Gorge and Leigh Woods', in *Archaeological*

Aspects of Woodland Ecology, ed. M. Bell and S. Limbrey, Br Archaeol Rep, Int ser 146 (Oxford), pp. 171–76.

Rahtz, P.A., 1982. 'The Dark Ages, 400–700 AD', in *The Archaeology of Somerset: a Review to 1500 AD*, ed. M. Aston and I. Burrow (Taunton), pp. 98–107.

Rahtz, P.A., 1991. 'Pagan and Christian by the Severn Sea', in *The Archaeology and History of Glastonbury Abbey: Essays in Honour of the Ninetieth Birthday of C.A. Raleigh Radford*, ed. L. Abrams and J.P. Carley (Woodbridge), pp. 3–37.

Rahtz, P.A., et al., 1992. *Cadbury Congresbury, 1968–73: a Late/Post-Roman Hilltop Settlement in Somerset*, Br Archaeol Rep, Br ser, 223 (Oxford).

Reade, R.C., 1885. 'The Roman villa at Great Wemberham in Yatton', *Proc Somerset Archaeol & Nat Hist Soc*, 31. ii, pp. 64–73.

Renfrew, A.C. and Level, E.V., 1979. 'Exploring dominance: predicting polities from centres', in *Transformations: Mathematical Approaches to Culture Change*, ed. C. Renfrew and K.L. Cooke (New York and London), pp. 145–67.

Rippon, S. 1991. 'The Somerset Levels in the Roman period', *Severn Estuary Levels Research Committee Annual Report* (Lampeter), pp. 43–6.

Rippon, S., 1992. 'The exploitation of the North Somerset Levels in the Roman period', *Severn Estuary Levels Research Committee Annual Report* (Lampeter), pp. 35–38.

Rippon, S., 1993. 'The Severn wetland during the historic period', *Severn Estuary Levels Research Committee Annual Report* (Lampeter), pp. 31–35.

Savory, J.H., 1924. 'The Tickenham rock shelter', *Proc Univ Bristol Spelaeol Soc*, 2. ii, pp. 173–75.

Scarth, H.M., 1873. 'The camps on the River Avon at Clifton', *Archaeologia*, 40, pp. 428–34.

Scarth, H.M., 1885. 'The Roman villa at Wemberham in Yatton', *Proc Somerset Archaeol & Nat Hist Soc*, 31, pp. 1–9.

Seyer, S., 1821. *Memoirs Historical and Topographical of Bristol.*

Smith, J.T., 1978. 'Halls or yards? A problem of interpretation', *Britannia*, 9, pp. 349–56.

Sykes, C.M., 1951. 'The Birdcombe villa, Wraxall, nr Bristol (an interim report)', *Proc Somerset Archaeol & Nat Hist Soc*, 96, pp. 234–35.

Sykes, C.M. and Brown, G.A., 1961. 'The Wraxall villa', *Proc Somerset Archaeol & Nat Hist Soc*, 105, pp. 37–51.

Tate, W.E., 1948, *Somerset Enclosure Acts and Awards* (Somerset Archaeol & Nat Hist Soc, Taunton).

Tatham, G., 1957. 'Environmentalism and possibilism', in *Geography in the Twentieth Century*, ed. T.G. Taylor, 3rd edn (London).
Taylor, C.C., 1989. 'Whittlesford: the study of a river-edge village', in *The Rural Settlements of Medieval England*, ed. M. Aston, D. Austin and C. Dyer, (Oxford), pp. 207–27.
Thomas, M., 1984. *The Book of Nailsea* (Buckingham).
Tylecote, R.F., 1977. 'Metallurgical remains', in *Gatcombe*, ed. K. Branigan (Oxford) pp. 125–27.
VCH Somerset 1. *The Victoria History of Somerset*, Vol. I. ed. W. Page. (London 1906).
VCH Somerset 2. *The Victoria History of Somerset*, Vol. 2, ed. W. Page. (London 1911).
Von Thünen, J.H., 1826. *Der Isolierte Staat in Beziehung auf Landwirtschaft und Nationalökonomie* (Rostock).
Watson, N.M., 1987. 'Excavations at Burwalls House, Bristol, 1980', *Bristol & Avon Archaeology*, 6, pp. 58–60.
Whitelock, D. (ed.) 1955. *English Historical Documents, c.500–1042* (London).
Wigan, E., n.d. *The Tale of Gordano* (Taunton).
Williams, E.H.D. and Gilson, R.G., 1981. 'Birdcombe Court, Wraxall', *Bristol Archaeol Res Group Rev*, no. 2,
Williams, M., 1964. 'Draining activity in the Somerset Levels since 1939', *Geography*, 44. iv, pp. 387–99.
Williams, M., 1970. *The Draining of the Somerset Levels* (Cambridge).

INDEX